Kindred Spirits: The Bonding of Religious and Laity

Maurice L. Monette. O.M.I.

Sheed & Ward

Back Cover Photo: Marc Boisvert

Sheed & Ward ^{TM} is a service of National Catholic Reporter Publishing Company, Inc.

Library of Congress Catalog Number: 87-61530

ISBN: 1-55612-070-2

Published by: Sheed & Ward
               115 E. Armour Blvd. P.O. Box 414292
               Kansas City, MO 64141-4292

To order, call: (800) 333-7373

CONTENTS

The Origin, Evolution and Assumptions of *Kindred Spirits*

Chapter I

Chapter II

Chapter III

Chapter IV

Kindred Spirits: The Bonding Of Religious And Laity

Dedication

In gratitude to the friends of 20 years in Intentional Christian Communities: Communitas (Washington, D.C.), NOVA (Arlington, VA.), The Community of John the Evangelist (New Orleans, LA.), The Woodstock Community (N.Y., N.Y.), The Natick Community (Natick, MA), and to my Aunts and Uncles: Beatrice Monette, S.A.S.V., Lorette Monette, S.A.S.V., Lucille Monette, S.A.S.V., Rita Monette, S.A.S.V., Leo C. Monette, O.M.I., Real LaBrie, O.M.I., Lionel LaBrie, O.M.I.

Acknowledgments

Books are rarely the product of a single mind or a single pen. Without the support and critique of many people, *Kindred Spirits* could never have been produced. I am grateful to all who in the last two years have shared with me their experiences and reflections: to those who responded to questionaires and telephone calls, to the authors of the books used in the footnotes, and to the many folk who expressed concern and interest in the project.

Kindred Spirits is a product of the Lay-Religious Bonding Project, sponsored since 1985 by the American Catholic Lay Network (Washington, D.C.). Joe Holland, the founder and director of the network, originated the idea that I research the phenomenon of lay-religious bonding, publish a report and disseminate the results through conferences. Thanks to his inspiration, the encouragement of the ACLN board and the support of staff members Peter Carter, Lisa Sosa, Maija Beattie, Emily Swartz, Mary Liepold and Bob Maxwell, the contribution which Joe and I once hoped to make to the church is now being realized.

Without a generous grant from the Missionary Oblates of Mary Immaculate (St. Jean Baptist Province), the project could not have even gotten off the ground. The Oblates provided all of the necessary funds required for two years of research and writing. I am most grateful to my brothers and to the two provincials who so generously committed our resources to this project: Maurice G. Laliberté and Donald W. Arel.

One of the greatest rewards received by an author is the careful critique of his work by his own peers. I am most grateful to those who shared so much of their time and energy with me: to Gail Bruch, Norman R. Comtois, O.M.I., Roland Faley, T.O.R., W. Harold Grant, Kenneth Hannon, O.M.I., Eugene Hemrick, Robert Heyer, Jean Marie Hiesberger, Joe Holland, Madonna Kolbenschlag, H.M., Dolores Leckey, Jean Lynch, S.B.S., James W. Maney, Lauretta Mather, S.S.S.F., Clarence C. Menard, O.M.I., Peggy Nichols, C.S.J., Arthur Powers and Brenda King-Powers, Lucien J. Richard, O.M.I., Frederick Sackett, O.M.I., Jeanne Schweickert, S.S.S.F., Sarah Marie Sherman, R.S.M., Loughlan Sofield, M.S., David J. Suley, and Mary David Walgenbach, O.S.B. These pastoral ministers, theologians, historians, canon lawyers, laity and religious are also, in a sense, the authors of *Kindred Spirits*.

The major draft of this book was written at the Oblate School of Theology in San Antonio, Texas. Grateful for their warm hospitality and professional support, I extend my thanks to President Patrick Guidon, O.M.I., Dean Robert Lampert, and to all of the school's professors, administrative staff and students.

Introduction

Something out of the ordinary is happening between Christian faithful and members of traditional religious communities. The faithful are requesting affiliation with these communities. They want to take part in the prayer and the simple communal lifestyle and they want to work with the poor.

The religious are responding in kind, opening their chapels, houses and workplaces—but not without some consternation! "How is it that youthful lay energies are attracted to traditional communities which twenty years ago were being pronounced dead?"

While the new lay energies for mission in the world and ministry to the church[1] are expanding into the traditional domain of the religious communities, the communities themselves are discovering new reasons for living and reclaiming their identities within the prophetic tradition of Christianity.

In the last ten years this phenomenon has sparked new life into at least half of the 900 U.S. religious communities and enriched the spirits of thousands of Christian faithful of all ages. International Liaison for Lay Volunteers in Mission, a brokering agency for international and domestic volunteer programs, estimates (conservatively) that in 1987 among their affiliates are 40 religious institutes which serve at least 275 lay missioners, most of them in their twenties and thirties. Surveys conducted for this book indicate that at least half of the over 500 religious institutes in the U.S. sponsor some kind of program for lay associates. Many of the other institutes express great interest or are actually in the process of forming associate or volunteer service programs.

Associate and volunteer programs are among the newer styles of collaboration between laity and religious. But such bonding is also taking place in other spheres: in the local church, in institutions and organizations, and in special efforts to foster lay mission and ministry.

(1) In the local church, laity are being supported in their ministry and spirituality by members of religious institutes who work in parishes and dioceses as pastors, directors of education, and pastoral ministers.

(2) Laity are being mobilized for ministry and mission by organizations created specifically for that purpose by religious institutes. Among such organizations are the Passionists' Center for Creative Ministries in Toronto, the Pallottine Center for Apostolic Development in Washington, D.C., and the Jesuits' Christian Life Communities based in Saint Louis.

(3) Lay spiritual and ministerial endeavors are being funded by religious institutes or supported by public commitments of those institutes to lay ministry or mission. The Oblates of Mary Immaculate, for instance, have established a fund for the training of lay ministers in the local churches served by their clergy in the Midwest. The same congregation is also funding this research project on bonding. Through the Pallottine Institute for Lay Leadership and Apostolate Research at

Seton Hall University in New Jersey, the Pallottines are funding a number of research projects on lay mission. Many lay organizations like the American Catholic Lay Network and the Chicago Call to Action are partially funded by religious institutes. These are only a few examples.

Such collaboration is certainly one of the most creative developments among Catholic religious orders in recent years. The significance of these emerging structural bonds between religious and laity is perhaps best understood in terms of the historical and social context. This context includes the following elements:

(1) The emphasis of the Second Vatican Council on the role of the laity in the modern world, including the universal call to holiness, ministry and mission.

(2) The numerical decline of members and recruits in religious institutes and the concommitant desire of religious to engage in work with and on behalf of the poor and to reform their institutions to better serve that purpose.

(3) The rise of lay spiritual energies as manifested in the explosion of lay ministry and leadership in the church; networks like the American Catholic Lay Network; organizations like the National Association for Lay Ministry; books, conferences and the Synod of 1987 exploring concerns about the relation between faith and work; political activity around social issues like abortion, the economy and peace; and the search for a properly lay spirituality.

(4) The quest for "community" evident in the growing attraction of community-conscious evangelical groups such as those referred to in a recent Vatican study, "Sects or New Religious Movements: A Pastoral Challenge" (May 1986). The document acknowledges that these groups prosper in part because they provide "human warmth, care and support in small close-knit communities" as well as "a style of prayer and

preaching closer to the cultural traits and aspirations of the people."
This very self-critical assessment of the church calls for a "rethinking, at
least in many local situations, of the traditional parish."

(5) The new context of Catholicism in the U.S.: the post-immigrant,
post-industrial church with an educated, monied, and politically influen-
tial laity.

These developments seem to be a gift of the Spirit for the renewal of
religious institutes and the laity. If this bonding is not nourished and
deepened, both religious and laity will lose a great opportunity for
deepening the power of the Gospel to heal the profound crises of our
society. The crucial question for those who belong to religious orders is
how to relate to the post-modern rise of lay spiritual energies. As Joe
Holland, Director of the American Catholic Lay Network, has written
in a letter addressed to provincials and leaders of religious institutes.

If the traditional orders ignore the fresh spiritual energies of
the laity, or still worse, are fearful or jealous of them, then both
religious and laity will suffer a great loss. The new lay movements will be deprived of the ancient spiritual wisdom and prophetic commitment embodied in the traditional orders. The
traditional orders will in turn be deprived of the youthful and
vibrant energies of the Spirit coming through the post-modern
laity.

There are a number of reasons for religious institutes to be concerned with the rise of lay energies:

(1) Institutes seeing the work of the Spirit in the rise of lay spiritual
energies are claiming to need involvement in these energies for their
own meaning and belonging. Institutes are rediscovering their rooted-
ness in the one baptism which all the faithful share.

(2) Institutes are asking how they can use their own resources for promoting the lay energies. This resourcing includes financial aid, support groups, ministerial leadership styles which empower lay leadership in church and society, and use of properties.

(3) Institutes are lacking personnel for staffing worthwhile ministries like parishes, retreat houses, schools and social services. They are asking whether they can provide for the continuance/transformation of these ministries and resources through lay people.

(4) Institutes know from history that their survival sometimes depends on the willingness to be "re-founded" in response to cultural crises within church and society. The present cultural crisis and the kind of re-founding response that it invites is, as explored in chapter three, intimately tied with the fundamental meaning of being Christian in the world.

There are also a number of reasons why Christian faithful feel kinship with the traditional religious communities:

(1) At a time when many Christians are enthusiastically seeking spiritual growth and community, religious institutes are treasure houses of spiritual disciplines, spiritual theologies, and community settings in which Christians can find common language with which to discern the movements of the Spirit.

(2) Religious institutes also have an accumulated wisdom to share about prophetic mission and ministry of the church.

(3) Religious institutes possess resources like properties, institutions, projects and monies which they are often eager to share with the emerging laity.

***

This book is divided into four chapters. Chapter I illustrates and explains each of the four major styles of bonding which were reported in two surveys conducted by the author in 1986. One study was directed to 500 provincials and leaders of religious institutes of men and women; another to 1500 members of the American Catholic Lay Network. Over four hundred verbal or written responses were received. The research did not pretend to be exhaustive or complete, just exploratory. Its purpose was merely to surface the major styles of bonding presently occurring between religious institutes and Christian faithful.

Chapters II and III place today's relationships between laity and religious within a broader historical and theological context. Chapter II is a primer on the history of "religious life" and of collaboration between religious and laity. It focuses on how the growth of religious community life and religious ideals at any one time in history is a response or reaction to changing social and ecclesial needs. The third chapter develops criteria for assessing the quality of relationships between laity and religious. These criteria are based on the new lay consciousness which has emerged within the context of the Second Vatican Council and on "the signs of the times" as read by the U.S. bishops.

Chapter IV explores the future of bonding, focusing especially on major trends and key issues.

This book was written for the benefit of laity and religious involved or about to be involved in collaborative relationships: for associates, volunteers in ministry, co-workers, temporary residents in religious houses, men and women religious, policy makers in both religious institutes and lay organizations, and for advocates of the poor. The book is a "primer." Its purpose is to "prime the pump," to surface the energy which has emerged through the collaboration of so many laity and religious. It tells of lessons learned, old traditions and new possibilities so that bonding between laity and religious may be better appreciated, better nurtured and better promoted.

Lay groups and religious communities can use *Kindred Spirits* as a guide for planning or evaluating lay-religious bonding efforts. To that end, the book includes (1) a framework for understanding the historical and theological significance of bonding and (2) a set of criteria for planning and evaluating collaborative projects. Discussion questions at the end of each of the four chapters provide an agenda for four or more meetings on the topic of lay religious bonding. These questions facilitate the personal integration of the material presented in each chapter and the application of the material to the collaborative relationships particular to the discussion group.

Volunteer, associate and co-worker groups which have been in existence for an extended period eventually face the question of how to initiate new members. *Kindred Spirits* is a useful tool for introducing new members to the historical and theological foundations of the church's prophetic and communal tradition. The four chapters and the discussion questions provide a framework for at least four discussions on how the group in which the members are being initiated fits into the church's tradition.

Like any other human work, *Kindred Spirits* is, in a sense, unfinished. The book answers a number of questions about the phenomenon of lay-religious bonding, but it also gives rise to others. One such is whether there exist other models of lay-religious bonding. Another is whether the concept of bonding does not equally apply to relationships between laity and priests. Most of the criteria developed in chapter three certainly apply to clergy-laity bonding; and readers of the initial draft have already begun to use them. But further research is needed into current models, history, major issues and trends. Concerning these and other questions pertaining to *Kindred Spirits*, the author would appreciate hearing from his reader.

Footnotes

1. "Ministry" refers to the ways in which Christians take care of each other and nurture each other for mission. "Mission" refers to the work of Christians in culture and society, including the home, the workplace, the marketplace, and the social and civic arena.

2. According to the Catholic Directory there are approximately 300 communities of men and 600 communities of women, if by communities we mean autonomous provinces, some of which belong to the same religious institute (e.g., O.F.M. Franciscans). The term "institute," as used in this book, is a generic term referring to what Canon Law calls the "institutes of consecrated life" and the "societies of apostolic life." "Institute," in other words, is used as an abbreviation for "institutes and societies." A more detailed explanation of the canonical categories is offered in a footnote in chapter two. For a discussion of the problems involved in calling religious institutes "religious communities," see chapter four.

1

Styles Of Bonding

Four Stories

Gail Bruch

"Kindly care" is the charism of the Sisters of Bon Secours. But it is also the charism of Gail Bruch, wife and mother of five children.

For the last four years Gail has been an Associate with the Sisters of Bon Secours, the congregation which runs the hospital where she works.

The relationship began when the Sisters invited Gail and several other hospital workers to participate in their mission, life and ministry. "My exposure to their charism which is partly centered around 'Kindly-Care,'" she says, "drew me to desire a deeper relationship with the Sisters. When offered the invitation of Associate Membership, I joyfully accepted."

Her family's initial reaction was one of support and it has continued to be so as her involvement has deepened. "My family accepts my Associate role as a way that I live out my spirituality. They recognize the importance of this in my life."

Gail's relationship with the Sisters through the Associate Program involves prayer, family gatherings, service to the suffering and the needy in the spirit of "Kindly Care." One morning every week at 7 a.m., she meets with a small group of Associates and Sisters to reflect over the past week. In hopes of increasing the awareness of God's presence in their lives, they reflect and listen to each other tell of the graced moments of the past week.

The small group joins the larger Associate group monthly, and every year joins with other Bon Secours Associate groups around the U.S. for a retreat.

Gail is participating in the Bon Secours Community's two-year study on "Justice." She is also contributing to the process of creating a new information program for Associate candidates.

Why does she choose to live out her Christian vocation under the auspices of Bon Secours? What does her association with the religious community add to her present service of God through her family, church, neighbors and community? The charism of "Kindly Care" drew her to the Sisters, with whom she has worked for twenty years. "My initial motive may have been in part a desire to grow in personal faith and deepen my relationship with God. Now, because I have grown through my association with the Sisters, I see that I can affect the lives of others through ministry dedicated to God and the service of humankind."

Her spiritual growth as an Associate even occasioned a change in her work-life. "Three years ago after extensive discernment I began Home Health Nursing on a part-time basis, along with my regular Nursing Supervisory position at the hospital. I have felt drawn to Home Health, ministering to patients and families on a one-to-one basis, and am better able to serve God's people as a Home Health Nurse."

There are other ways in which her life has changed. "Due to my association with this religious community, I have experienced heightened awareness of Christian purpose in many issues I face as wife, mother and professional. I am concerned about many justice issues such as the proper care of AIDS patients and the education of the public for more generous response to the victims. I am also concerned about health care to the elderly and poor; and I am struggling to find ways to compensate for the policies which regulate and limit the care provided. My experience with the Bon Secours Community provides the impetus to grow in the faith and strength that I need to explore and act on these and other issues in my everyday life."

The relationship has been positive for the Sisters too, she says. By sharing more deeply in the struggles of lay men and women like herself they have been affirmed in their belief that the Church is the People of God. They are even being reminded of the roots of their own congregation. In 1821, the first Sisters of Bon Secours began home care for the sick in Paris. One hundred years later, after becoming identified with the hospitals they founded, the Sisters are welcoming Associates like Gail, some of whom are pursuing the congregation's original work.

> "My relationship with the Sisters has had a very powerful effect on my life. Hopefully I am extending the Kingdom of God through sharing in the mission and charism of Bon Secours. This is what binds me to association with a religious community."

W. Harold Grant

"What is it like to be a lay person in a community which includes vowed religious?" I asked.

"Do you come from a large family?" he asked.

"No."

"It's like a large family. We have our share of fussing and also our share of love."

For no less than 38 years W. Harold Grant has been a member of the Missionary Cenacle Apostolate and is now the General Custodian of that group and the Director of the Missionary Cenacle Volunteers, a program sponsored by the Missionary Cenacle Family. The Missionary Cenacle Family includes sisters (Missionary Servants of the Most Blessed Trinity), brothers and priests (Missionary Servants of the Most Holy Trinity), members of a pious union (Blessed Trinity Institute), as well as laity (Missionary Cenacle Apostolate). Each of these form an independent branch of the Family.

Dr. Grant belongs to the lay branch. Each month he meets with other men and women of his local Missionary Cenacle to pray, discuss their apostolic works, and to make community decisions. Members live in their own homes with their own families and pursue their own employment to support themselves and their families. Dr. Grant worked for twenty-five years as a university professor and administrator.

The Missionary Cenacle Apostolate, he says, is on an upswing. Since 1982 membership has increased from about 500 to almost 900 and many new local communities called Missionary Cenacles have been established.ed He attributes the upswing to a recovery of their original charism. The road has been difficult at times. After Vatican II, membership declined from 2000 to about 500 and many local communities dissolved. Influenced by the Council's People of God ecclesiology and its theology of the laity, the Family has struggled to redefine its relationships. Many of the lay members who rejected the "laity helping Father and Sister" mentality left as did some who did not want that mentality taken away from them.

In the process, the Missionary Cenacle Apostolate has rediscovered the charism of its founder. Fr. Thomas A. Judge, C.M., had originally gathered, not sisters, brothers and priests, but lay men and women.

Their association was aimed precisely at nurturing the ministry of the laity in the mission of the Church in family, work, leisure and society. Theirs was to be an apostolate especially to the abandoned.

Dr. Grant believes that the present growth of the Missionary Cenacle Apostolate is a result of this rediscovery of the group's basic charism. The members are re-aligning their relationships with the other branches of the Family while pursuing their own ministries in society to the most abandoned. He speaks with great pride about his Cenacle's efforts to respond to local needs. "Our apostolate is by design not in the mainstream institutional setting. We look for those who are not in the mainstream and whose needs are not met by the mainstream. We have to be careful not to be assimilated into mainstream structures. So, we who work with the abandoned often feel abandoned ourselves. But that is our unique mission."

Arthur Powers and Brenda King-Powers

On the night they received the death threat, Brenda and Arthur Powers reassured their neighbors that they would be fine and that, no, there would be no need for the neighbors to stay in the house with them that night. Upon arising the next morning, the Powers were touched to learn that throughout the night the neighbors had taken turns standing guard at their doorstep.

The Powers' have been threatened more than once since they volunteered as Franciscan lay missionaries in the village of Caseara in the Brazilian interior state of Goias. Arthur and Brenda serve in this rural community as pastoral ministers, facilitating base communities, organizing and leading liturgy, teaching, counseling, and gathering the Christian community around local needs. They are responsible to and are supported by a Franciscan priest who visits the community once a month for Eucharist and Reconciliation.

Death threats are not directed arbitrarily to Church workers. They are directed to those who like the Powers have crossed a certain line in their ministry. Arthur and Brenda crossed it when they acted on their analysis that a major root cause of the problems in their community, was the problem of land tenure or the ownership of farmland.

My wife and I did not come to this part of Brazil to work with land issues. We came as pastoral workers, responsible for the administration of a sub-parish: catechism, sacramental preparation, base community groups, health and family problems— the whole gamut of parish life. We began to dis cover the major pastoral problems: hunger, malnutrition, unemployment, family breakups, alcoholism. Listening to the people in their homes and in small group meetings, we gently probed for the causes of these problems. We discovered that over the last fifteen years, hundreds of families had left the land, many of them illegally defrauded, some of them threatened or forced. Fathers were no longer able to support their families, or had to spend weeks away from home as poorly paid prospectors or day laborers. In our village people are going hungry while all around us are vast expanses of unused land.

With that understanding, Arthur and Brenda began several ministries in tandem with the Land Commission of the Brazilian Conference of Catholic Bishops: defending the small farmers, encouraging them to organize unions, and raising the community's consciousness about Church teaching regarding the proper use of the earth's resources.

Waiting for Arthur and Brenda on the other side of the line were the wealthy landowners, speculators and corporations. As land is becoming more valuable and tax incentives more attractive, these wealthy interests are buying huge tracts of land which are already inhabited by small farmers who have possessory rights to the land without legal title. At the same time, poor rural workers with no means of supporting their families are occupying unused or underused land owned by these wealthy interests and are staking out possessory claims.

Their story is now the story of many Brazilian Church workers who, having made a clear option for the poor, stand with the homesteaders and small farmers who refuse to abandon to the wealthy their rightful place on the land.

This may seem to be a strange situation in which to find two U.S. citizens who once worked in corporate, international law and in community development. But, Arthur and Brenda decided that joining the Franciscans in Brazil would be a more meaningful way to expend their energies and raise their two adopted daughters.

Brenda and Arthur met in Brazil while both were members of the peace Corps. They returned after getting married and completing their education. In Rio de Janeiro, Brenda worked as a community organizer while Arthur pursued a law practice with international corporations. They had returned to the U.S. and had settled around Boston when their calling to live and work in rural Brazil insisted itself anew. The Franciscans with whom they had been working in a soup kitchen invited Arthur and Brenda to consider joining them in their Brazilian missions as lay missionaries. A contract was drawn based on that of the Maryknoll Lay Associates, clearly one of the most developed programs in the U.S.

Arthur and Brenda are quite pleased with their contract. They are committed to the Brazilian missions for three years with option to renew indefinitely for three year periods. They are given room andboard and paid a small salary directly by the Franciscans. In Arthur's words, they are able to save a little for the future because one just doesn't spend money in poverty-stricken Caseara where it is considered extravagant to buy a beer. According to the contract, after six years of service, Brenda and Arthur are eligible to receive college tuition grants for their children as well as retirement benefits for themselves. Art, Brenda and the two girls expect to be missionaries well into the future. It's a vocation for them.

Mary David Walgenbach

What happens when a traditional religious community realigns its relationship to other religious groups so that, metaphorically, being "at the center" is not as important as being "in the circle?" Sr. Mary David Walgenbach knows about circles, centers of circles, and being with others in a circle. The metaphor clearly reflects her own lifestyle at the Saint Benedict Center in Madison, WI.

The Center has been in existence since 1966. It was founded by the Madison Benedictine Women in response to needs voiced by clergy of all faiths and other people in Madison. Since then, the ecumenical Center has hosted a variety of activities, including retreats and workshops on topics like spirituality, liturgy and peacemaking. Many circles of people call the Center home, says Sr. Mary David.

In 1980, the local Benedictine community committed themselves to a group of laypeople searching for the meaning of religious "community life." They began to meet with each other regularly, every two or three weeks, to share a meal, listen to speakers, discuss their personal journeys and pray. The group was composed of 20 people from several separate households. When the time came to choose leadership, the groups "naturally" turned to the sisters.

But, the sisters refused! At this pivotal moment, the sisters opted not to be the center of the community but one among the many households in the community; in the circle with others, but not the center as such. The Community of Benedict, unlike many "associate programs," does not revolve around the religious institute. This optionhas shaped the future of Mary David Walgenbach and that of the Community of Benedict and the other ventures at the Saint Benedict Center.

The Community clearly draws inspiration from the Benedictine tradition, but that tradition contributes to the Community along side the other religious traditions of its members. The Community is ecumenical and varied in lifestyle, including married people, single people, elderly and children. The Benedictine sisters are one household among others in this circle that they call the Community of Benedict.

Since 1980, Sr. Mary David Walgenbach and her other Benedictine companion, Sr. Joanne Kollasch have helped form yet other circles, including a resident community and a monastic school. The "resident community" is a group of eight people, including the sisters, who have committed themselves to each other in pursuit of religious "community life" at St. Benedict Center. They are in the process of covenanting themselves to a vowed life together, within the monastic tradition, on a lifelong basis, sharing their goods. Their membership, like that of the Community of Benedict, is varied. It includes two married couples, one being Quaker and Methodist in background, the other, Catholic; a single Jewish man who lives the Quaker tradition; a woman who is widowed and Presbyterian; and the two Benedictine sisters. Their community is composed of five separate households and at least six different religious traditions! Together they seek "to obey God in community" by studying Scripture, praying, discerning the experiences of the group, seeking the signs of the times, and entering into dialogue with people of other traditions. Several times each week they share meals, study and work.

The resident community has taken on as one of its ministries the creation of a monastic school, a refuge for people seeking renewal of the heart. Begun in the Fall of 1987, the "resident program," as it is called, accepts 15 to 20 adults from a variety of backgrounds, for the duration of three 10-week semesters each year. The daily schedule includes manual work, common meals, worship, and study as well as mo ments of silence and solitude. The five or six seminars offered each term focus on personal and social transformation through the study of spirituality (including the contemplative traditions of the Hasidic Jews, the

Quakers and the Benedictines), Scripture and other sacred writings, feminist theology and literature, the dynamics of community, non-violent social change, vocational decision-making, and the arts of writing, weaving and poetry.

As the literature on the resident program explains:

> We live in a society that does not need people with new skills and new information as much as it needs people with new hearts. The aim of the Resident Program is nothing less than heart renewal. We want participants to return to work, neighborhood, family, school, not with a new diploma but with a new presence, a presence that makes for justice and peace... it is the aim of our entire life together to allow the work of the spirit to be done in us and among us—the spirit that is always "making all things new" in our hidden selves and, through us, in our communities and our world.

The kind of community living Sr. Mary David experiences daily at St. Benedict Center is reminiscent of the 19th century American Shaker villages and of certain seventh century monastic experiments (e.g., the family monasteries of St. Fructuosus). It hardly resembles the traditional community life of the Benedictine sisters. How, I asked, does one reconcile being a Benedictine and living in such a radically different type of community?

> We Benedictines have one way of looking at life and living in community. These people also bring authentic ways of living and looking at life. Together we are trying to come up with a community that can be lifegiving for such a diversified group most of whom are lay people. Benedict himself, you know, originally founded the community for lay people. Besides, hospitality toward strangers has always been a Benedictine trait.

Living in such a mixed community seems to give life to her commitment as a religious:

> I really feel that this is where I want to be. It energizes me. This kind of community is more reflective of the church than a community composed totally of celibate women. The diversity has added a great richness to my life. I feel that we are part of an experiment through which the Spirit is leading us. We are trying to stay open to the Spirit and not control the outcome.

What will religious life (in the monastic tradition) look like in the future? Sr. Mary David imagines a proliferation of communities not unlike her own: diverse groups of people in one place where people of different ages, lifestyles and religions can live together and share in a commom vision that supports diversity and some form of sharing of that gift with the outside world.

Sr. Mary David addressed many other issues during our conversation, issues too complex to elaborate here. But she always returned to her core message about how important it is "...to be at home on the circle, knowing that one spot on the circle is important and that being there links us with other people."

The Reported Styles of Bonding

Gail, Harold, Arthur, Brenda and Mary David are a few of the many ardent Christians whose spiritual quest is quickened by the fact that they have chosen to stand at the juncture of two contemporary movements: the purification of traditional "religious life" and the emergence of the laity. Like giant plates grinding below the surface of the earth, these movements are releasing ancient spiritual energies for the laity and religious who dare to live together on the edge.

The stories of Gail, Harold, Arthur, Brenda and Mary David are a sampling of the many ways in which religious and laity are bonding at this juncture of history. The following pages explore the major styles of bonding or spiritual kinship which laity and religious have reported in two surveys. This overview of "what is happening" will prepare the way for a deeper look at the historical and theological roots of bonding in chapters two and three.

Chart I
Bonding Styles

Foreign and domestic volunteers

Volunteers working side by side with members of religious institutes, for a temporary period, among the poor at-home or abroad.

Associates

Formally recognized associates to a religious institute, relating to the community in several ways, sometimes distinct, often overlapping.

Associates in prayer and support

People sharing prayer, correspondence, financial contributions and occasional meetings with institute members.

Associates in community living

People living in the house of a religious institute while working with the members or while pursuing studies or work elsewhere.

Associates in spiritual formation

People who identify with an institute's charism and wish to be nurtured spiritually and intellectually in order to live that charism in their own ministry.

Members of a religious family

Lay people being full members of a religious "family" and having their own organizational structures distinct from those of the sisters, brothers or priests with whom they are related.

Co-workers in ministry

People who work with members of a religious institute (in some established ministry of the institute or in some commonly shared project) and cultivate together a sense of mission and spirituality according to or consistent with the charism and tradition of the institute.

Chart I summarizes the four major styles of bonding which were reported by religious and laity around the U.S. Each of these represents a characteristic way in which laity and religious relate to each other: as volunteers, as associates, as members of a religious family, or as co-workers. This chapter explores each of the styles in detail.

The four styles are a humble attempt to describe and categorize relationships which in fact are impossible to define with any rigidity. Relationships are fluid. Styles of relating change and overlap. Like all efforts at theoretical modeling, this chart is merely a guide to understanding complex relationships.

How, for instance, is one to categorize Gail's relationship with the Sisters of Bon Secours? She is a "co-worker" at the hospital, but she is also, in a sense, an "associate in spiritual formation" if not also an "associate in prayer and support." I classify her primarily as a co-worker because she relates most consistently with the sisters and the other associates in her capacity as a hospital worker.

There are also a number of motives or ends for which Gail might wish to bond with the sisters and the other associates: at times she and the sisters relate for growth in mission and ministry; at others, for prayer and support; at yet other times, for spiritual formation. Gail does not actually live with the sisters, but other women do. Most likely, the primary focus of their relationship is community living.

Each of the styles of bonding represents a different configuration of motives or ends. Volunteers bond primarily for mission and ministry. Associates bond very often for prayer and support, sometimes for spiritual development, and less often for community living. Associates may also nurture each other for mission and ministry and may even, like co-workers, engage in ministry projects together. Although focused primarily on their common ministry, co-workers may bond for spiritual formation as well as for prayer and support of their ministry beyond the workplace.

Lay members of a "religious family" may bond primarily around any of the above, depending on the particular charism of the family. Generally, contemplative families bond for prayer; apostolic families, for ministry. Chart II illustrates the four major focal points for bonding.

Chart II
Focal Points for Bonding

mission and ministry
prayer and support
spiritual formation
community living

Features of Bonding

Not every relationship between religious and laity is effective "bonding" in the sense used in this book (when, for instance, an associate program's major goal is to recruit members for the religious community). Chapter III elaborates a set of criteria for effective bonding. In brief, effective bonding is recognized by these general features:

(1) The laity involved are not trying to become sisters, brothers or priests; and the religious are not trying to recruit them. The laity are pursuing their own call to holiness, mission and ministry as Christians who are not members of religious institutes.

(2) The religious involved are not trying to become laity. Actually, they are laity! Vatican II clearly speaks of women and men religious (that is, those who are not clerics) as laity sharing the same baptism and relationship to the church. What distinguishes religious in the bonding relationship is their membership in particular institutes and their participation in the "community life movement" which has been part of the church practically since the beginning. More will be said about the various types of religious institutes and their history in the next chapter.

(3) The bonding relationship occurs within the context of other relationships to which both parties have primary commitments. Mothers and fathers, like Arthur and Brenda, have prior duties to each other and to their children just as religious have basic duties toward their communities. Single persons may not have specific formal commitments at a given time, but their choice has been to remain free and that choice is respected by the bonding relationship.

(4) Because of prior commitments and perhaps personal needs, the religious and laity involved usually relate on a temporary basis. Arthur and Brenda, for instance, commit themselves to their missionary work in Brazil for three-year periods. Harold's year by year commitment has practically become, after 37 years, a lifetime commitment! In any case, people who bond do not necessarily see each other every day, nor do they necessarily count on a commitment from each other which will last a lifetime. Often, they mutually agree to participate in certain activities or to be available to each other for a defined period of time.

Assuming these general features, the following pages explain each of the bonding styles in more detail.

Associates

The particular style of bonding which we call "associates" gained popularity only in the last ten years. More than half of the religious institutes surveyed for this book reported having or expressed interest in starting some sort of associate group.

The associate groups should not be identified with the traditional auxiliaries and guilds like the Association of Marian Helpers sponsored by the Marian Fathers or the OMI's Missionary Association of Mary Immaculate. These are "spiritual benefit societies" to promote vocations, raise funds, foster particular spiritual devotions, and encourage spiritual perfection. In a sense, these societies operated under a spiritual "trickle down" theory. Laity were to benefit spiritually from supporting in some way the "higher state of perfection" represented by the religious orders. These societies operated under the pre-Vatican II theologies of laity and religious life.

On the contrary, the new associate relationships between laity and religious are a mutual sharing with the purpose of deepening the spiritual life of both religious and lay (as well as clerical) associates. In the most successful of the associate relationships, this mutuality is enhanced by the common interest of the associates in the particular spirit of the religious institute and the charism of its foundress/founder. The associates share the institute's spiritual and ministerial heritage while maintaining their respective vocation, be it lay or religious.

Lay associates are known by several names: friends of the congregation, auxiliary members, co-members, associates or affiliates. Lay associations include women and/or men, single, married or clergy, Protestants and Jews as well as Catholics, and often former members of the institute. Some memberships include all of the above, some only certain categories. [1] Usually associates are already friends of the institute.

Most institutes require the associate to be in stable emotional condition and ascertain this through interviews.

Usually lay associates relate directly to the members of the religious institute with no separate and distinct organizational structure of their own. One member of the institute often serves as a sponsor or regular contact person, sometimes even as spiritual director or companion. The lay associate relationship is non-canonical and almost always excludes the formal right to vote on internal matters pertaining to the canonical institute.

Associates and institute members seek mutual enrichment and solidarity through prayer, study, ministry and recreation. The Ursulines of Mt. Maple, KY, for example, have several levels of involvement: one being prayer and concern; another, ministerial service on an occasional basis; and yet another, ministerial service on a regular basis. The Sisters of the Holy Cross also have three levels of association: one involving prayer, retreats and a newsletter; another involving participation in an instructional program in the institute's spiritual tradition as applied to one's own Christian lifestyle—including retreats, shared prayer, theological enrichment and celebrations; and another involving service in mission by contract.

There are several types of association. Here we classify them according to focus:

(1) Associates in prayer and support. People sharing prayer, correspondence, financial contributions and occasional meetings and celebrations with the members of the institute.[2]

(2) Associates in community living. People living in a religious institute community while working with the institute or while pursuing studies or work elsewhere. Residents must usually be financially independent, over 21, able to pay for their room and board as mutually agreed. In some cases, "residents" live alone, in which case they are expected to

live geographically close enough to participate in the community's activities.[3] The residents in Sr. Mary David's community at St. Benedict Center have gone further than most; they have formed a non-canonical, ecumenical religious community which includes two Benedictine Sisters.

(3) Associates in spiritual formation. People who associate with the members of an institute because they share in the institute's charism and wish to be nurtured in their properly lay mission by the spirit and resources of the institute.[4]

Many associate groups have developed certain procedures such as an initial interview, a formation program,[5] a probation period, a commitment liturgy, periodic evaluation, and an agreement that either party may sever the relationship at any time.

Most lay associates relate to women's institutes. A study by the National Conference of Religious Vocation Directors shows that 55 institutes of men and 132 institutes of women have lay associate programs and that 22 of men and 51 of women have programs for lay volunteers. Extended memberships in institutes of men are less common.[6] Perhaps this phenomenon is due to the clerical nature of most institutes of men. The relatively common theology which conceives of priests as a caste set apart can certainly hinder equality and dialogue with "associates." Perhaps a cultural factor is at play also. Male groups may be less likely to exhibit the nurturing and dialogical qualities characteristic of associate relationships. Another factor may be that the communities of men are generally more determined by their commitments to institutional maintenance of parishes and various types of schools. Perhaps women's communities are freer to bond with other Christians in non-traditional ways because their financial security is less tied to the traditional clerical structures. In any case, it is obvious that institutes of men are less likely to sponsor associate groups and more likely to sponsor volunteer programs.

Foreign and Domestic Volunteers

Volunteer programs connected to religious institutes have proliferated so rapidly in recent years that two major organizations have been established to broker volunteer relationships. International liaison of Lay Volunteers in Mission is a national organization that networks foreign and domestic volunteer program directors and provides information for volunteers. It sponsors lay mission information centers in Washington, D.C. and in St. Louis, MO and publishes yearly a directory of lay volunteer opportunities called *The Response* and a *Lay Mission Handbook*. There are also five Saint Vincent Pallotti Centers For Apostolic Development throughout the U.S. which broker information to the public about lay volunteer service opportunities. These centers, sponsored by the Society of the Catholic Apostolate (the Pallottines), annually publish a directory of service opportunities called *Connections*.

The brokers are being flooded with volunteers. In 1986 International Liaison reported an average of 300 to 400 inquiries each month! Who are they? Volunteers are mainly persons in their twenties and early thirties. Among these are professionals and students, international participants,[7] men and women, single and married, and some families.

Sponsorship of a particular program may be assumed by a religious institute on several levels: a local religious house, a province, a group of provinces,[8] or several religious institutes.[9]

Religious institutes sponsor volunteer programs for a variety of reasons, but the most common is to deepen vocations to the Christian (lay) way of life. Some institutes use volunteer programs for recruitment purposes. Volunteers are assisted in discerning a call to membership.[10] Yet other institutes recognize explicitly that some lay Christians have a call to be missionaries. The Society for African Mission Fathers in the Liberian missions, for instance, work side by side with lay Catholics pursuing their own professions or vocations while helping the priests to build and establish churches.

Some volunteers seek short term positions of one summer to one year; while others, especially those with a missionary vocation of some sort, seek long term commitments of two or three years or more. Most volunteer programs offer community living, a simple lifestyle, work among the economically poor, opportunities for group reflection on the experience, inclusion in the prayer and leisure life of a religious community. The work options are multiple: community organization, pastoral ministry, social work, and work in hospitals, soup kitchens, hospices, youth programs, education, etc. Housing is usually provided. Volunteers room in the house of a religious institute[11] or in a lay community house.[12] Among the other perks usually provided are training, post-volunteer job placement,[13] stipends, health insurance, transportation, on-site supervision and reflection on ministerial experience.

Among the most well-documented programs are the Mercy Corps, the Holy Cross Associates, and the Maryknoll Associate Lay Missioners. Volunteer programs, of course, vary in quality and stability. The following are among the most highly regarded by organizers. In the category of domestic programs: there are the Jesuit Volunteer Corps, the Mercy Corps, the Daughters of Charity Associates in Mission, theMissionary Cenacle Volunteers, the Claretian Lay Missionaries, the Pallottine Apostolic Associates, the Marianist Voluntary Service Communities, the Vincentian Service Corps, and the Sisters of Saint Joseph Associates in Mission. In the category of foreign programs: there are the Maryknoll Associate Lay Missioners and the Jesuit International Volunteers.

There are, of course, other volunteer programs which are not sponsored or linked to religious institutes. These include diocesan-sponsored programs like the Texas Catholic Conference's Volunteers for Educational and Social Services and the Los Angeles Archdiocese's Lay Mission-Helpers Association; and lay-sponsored programs like the Volunteer Missionary Movement and Lamp Ministries of New York City.

Co-workers in Ministry

There seem to be two distinct types of co-worker collaboration: collaboration between lay and religious co-workers in established ministries, like hospitals and schools owned and run by the religious; and collaboration between lay and religious co-workers in projects that are owned and run commonly by both. Examples of this second type are Connective Ministries, Peacework Alternatives, and the BostonCatholic Women. Connective Ministries is a network of church workers in solidarity with poor people in the American South.[14] Peacework Alternatives "is a national organization which encouragesdiscussion of the ethical aspects of defense work, seeks to provide a network of services for defense workers in struggle and works toward economic conversion."[15] Boston Catholic Women is a group of laywomen and sisters who meet monthly in prayer and solidarity to facilitate dialogue, education and positive action on issues of sexism, racism, classism and militarism.[16] There are many other lay-religious projects of this type, including peace groups like Catholics Against Nuclear Arms (Rochester, N.Y. area) and Witness for Peace at AVCO (Boston, MA area).

The rationale behind the quest for greater collaboration between religious and lay co-workers arises from several sources:

(1) Empirically, there are a growing number of ministries owned and administered by the institutes that rely heavily on the laity who work side by side with the institute members. The Jesuits of the Wisconsin Province, for instance, estimate that their staffs are 95% laity. Surely that is true of many other institutes in teaching and nursing ministries. As their membership and hence their labor-pool decreases, some religious institutes are choosing to employ more lay people rather than close their institutions. Likewise, the projects commonly shared by religious and laity reflect the empirical fact that certain tasks require a combination of skills and resources which neither group can muster alone.

(2) Theologically, collaboration in ministry is a recognition of the church's renewed understanding of the interdependence of the members of Christ's Body, and of each member's call to holiness and to ministry in the church and to the world.

(3) Organizationally, religious institutes are recognizing that effective collaboration in the ministries of their institutions (especially schools and hospitals) requires some common goals and assumptions. While diversity in perspective is healthy, too much can be destructive of an institution. Hence the need for religious and lay co-workers to explore shared values and vision about their work. Such sharing touches upon the role of the church, the relationship of the church to culture and society, the ultimate goals of the institution in which they work, and the moral issues which arise in the workplace.

In projects shared by both religious and lay folk, the same organizational need holds true. In fact, such projects as Boston Catholic Women tend to respond to that need more forcefully because of the necessity of shared vision and strategy for their very survival.

In keeping with this empirical, theological and organizational rationale, the nurturing of collaboration in the institutions of religious institutes has taken several forms including the following:

—the inclusion of laity on boards and advisory groups;[17]
—the sponsoring of weekend retreats for co-workers;[18]
—the issuance of formal statements by chapters of religious institutes in support of lay mission and ministry;[19]
—the inclusion of laity in foreign mission work on a long term basis.[20]

Religious Families

The tradition of lay membership in religious institutes extends back to the older monastic tradition of lay brothers and sisters (oblates) and to the fraternities, sororities, and early Third Orders of the mendicants. As we shall see in the next chapter, the Benedictines, Franciscans, Dominicans and Carmelites, for instance, gathered groups of laity who commited themselves to live the monastic or mendicant traditions in-the-world outside the walls of the monasteries or priories to the best of their abilities. Having adapted themselves to the needs of the times, some of these groups still exist today.

Oblates and Third Orders were defined by the 1919 Code of Canon Law as groups which pursue a papally approved rule under the direction and spirit of a religious order (Canon 702).

In recent times, in the spirit of Vatican II, such groups are conceived less as watered-down versions of religious life and more as secular or lay vocations. The revised Code of Canon Law calls some of these groups "Secular Institutes" and categorizes them under "Institutes of Consecrated Life" along with Religious Institutes. These Secular Institutes are by definition institutes of consecrated life in which Christians living in the world seek the perfection of charity and work for the sanctification of the world, especially from within.

In a different vein, certain religious institutes founded in more recent times include laity as members of their religious "family" as it were. Among these are the Missionary Cenacle Family, the Family of Mary (Marianists), and the Dominicans. These religious families include canonically recognized institutes of men and women and non-canonical associations of lay persons.[21]

The story of Dr. Harold Grant illustrates how lay persons participate in these religious families: the lay membership is organized into a non-canonical, self-governing branch of the family. While remaining true to its lay character, the lay branch shares a charism and mission with the other branches.

Discussion Questions

1. This chapter begins with several illustrations of lay-religious collaboration. Tell your own story: what relationships with laity (if you are

a religious) or with religious (if you are a lay person) have been most significant for you?

2. Which of the bonding styles have you experienced? Have you experienced other styles not mentioned in this chapter?

3. What did you learn from your collaborative relationships? What were the high points and low points of these relationships?

4. What kinds of collaborative relationships might you (and your group) envision for the future?

Footnotes

1. The Maryknoll Lay Missioner Program, for instance, includes laity as well as religious and clergy. Several institutes have associations specifically for former members, e.g., Maryknoll Sisters' "Full Circle Network" and the Congregation of Divine Providence program for former members.

2. E.g., the Holy Cross Sisters and Sisters of the Immaculate Heart of Mary.

3. E.g., the Immaculate Heart of Mary Sisters, Fransiscan Sisters of Dubuque, Mercy Sisters of Rochester and Pittsburgh, Sisters of Charity of Mt. St. Joseph in OH, LaSalette Fathers in Enfield, NH., the Oblates of Mary Immaculate in Willimantic, CT.

4. E.g., the Sisters of Mercy in Hartford, Dominican Sisters, Franciscan Sisters, Holy Cross Sisters, Ursulines of Louisville, Saint Joseph Sisters (CSJ) of Baden, Benedictines at Glastonbury Abbey and at Erie, PA.

5. E.g., the Sisters of St. Joseph of Cleveland.

6. E.g., the Salvatorians, Dominicans, Franciscans, Norbertines of DePere WI, the Missionaries of the Sacred Heart.

7. E.g., the Columban Fathers' Lay Volunteer Program.

8. E.g., the Sisters of Mercy provinces sponsor the Mercy Corps; and the Jesuit provinces, the Jesuit Volunteer Corps and the Jesuit International Volunteers.

9. E.g., the Vincentian Fathers and the Daughters of Charity together sponsor the Vincentian Service Corps.

10. E.g., the OFM Conventuals in Marytown and the Glenmary Sisters.

11. E.g., the Sisters of Saint Francis's Francis House in Baltimore.

12. E.g., the Edmundites, the Vincentians and the Daughters of Charity Service Corps.

13. E.g., the Pallottines and the Mill Hill Missionaries.

14. The nature and purpose of Connective Ministries: "We seek to encourage grass-roots empowerment efforts by developing linkages between local organising groups, providing opportunities for shared reflection among church workers, and connecting unorganized poor people with resource groups. We also seek to publicize the oft-ignored stories of struggling poor people. Our work is supported by contributions from religious orders, parishes and individuals." A description quoted in "CONNECTIVE MINISTRIES, 1985 ANNUAL REPORT AND EVALUATION" (P.O. Box 2892, Rock Hill, South Carolina 29731).

15. Peacework Alternatives, 3940 Poplar Level Road, Louisville, KY 40213

16. Boston Catholic Women, Box 593, East Boston, MA 02128

17. E.g., the Xaverian Brothers' schools and the St. Louis Priory Society of the Benedictine Fathers in MO.

18. E.g., the Marist Fathers and the Oblates of Mary Immaculate of the Central Province.

19. Such as the recognition by the Salesians that "the Salesian vocation is 'Salesian' before it is 'Religious'. This also means that the Salesian charism extends beyond the limits of the Congregation." The lay person who works with the congregation's spirit and in its apostolate is thereby considered a true "Salesian-in-the-world," a Christian living out a vocation to holiness in the work for youth in the spirit of Don Bosco. (Quote taken from a public statement sent by the Salesians to the author.)

20. E.g., the Society of African Missions has formed an Associates in Mission program for laity who would like to work with them in the missions. The S.M.A. Associates

in Mission join the society on a long term or life basis as lay missioners doing properly lay work. The program is still in formation stage with two lay people in Liberia.

21. The Missionary Cenacle Family includes a secular institute as well.

2

A Tradition Received:
Religious Life

Shapes From the Past

The contemporary decline in numbers of men and women in U.S. religious institutes should come as no surprise to the historians among us. Religious groups in the church have never been fixed, static entities firmly resisting the tides of history. The groups that are familiar to us today are part of a great movement which began in the early centuries of the church's existence and evolved through no less than five major ages.

According to the authors of a popular study of the religious life movement, each of these ages: (1) was inspired by some dominant image of religious life; (2) was responsive to or otherwise shaped by major developments in society and the church; and (3) was subject to a succession of phases: growth, decline, change-over to a new dominant image, and new growth under the new image.[1]

Struggle, despair, pain and hope accompanied each of these transitions into a new age. During the present transition, the U.S. church should expect no less, especially given the fact that this transition is the very first which this church has ever experienced on its own shores.

The present chapter delves into the history behind the present transition. It explores, in summary form, each of the major transitions of religious life, concentrating especially on the later transition which had

---

Ages in the History of Religious Life

Desert Asceticism 200-500 A.D.
Monasticism 500-1200 A.D.
Mendicant Orders 1200-1500 A.D.
Apostolic Orders 1500-1800 A.D.
Teaching Congregations 1800-Present

---

such an impact on the founding and growth of the U.S. church. Special attention is given to the role of lay persons in the evolution of religious life and to the earlier forms of lay-religious bonding.

The value of knowing history is that it can reveal to us the dangers and opportunities inherent to our present situation. History uncovers patterns in human and organizational behavior which promote understanding, obviate mistakes and offer hope for our children. The present chapter examines each of the five ages with an eye to the shape which religious life is taking in the present century and the ways in which all members of the church, including the faithful and members of religious institutes and societies, might collaborate more closely in living life more religiously.

The Five Ages

The Age of the Desert (200-500 A.D.)

In the first two centuries of the church, religious life was in a sense the ordinary life of the church. The church (numbering about 20,000 in 100 A.D.) then as now was shaped by the desire to provide an organized and systematic pursuit of holiness, while awaiting the final coming of Christ. Even in those early centuries, however, there were Christians who organized their pursuit of holiness in extraordinary ways. These were the consecrated widows and virgins who lived in small groupings and became renowned during the time of the church persecutions for their generous works and/or their secluded lives of prayer and asceticism.

The first emergence of religious life as we know it today occurred around the time when Christianity became established in the Roman Empire, sometime between the years 250 and 300. Lay men and women fled into the desert to pursue the ideal of life set by holy ascetics like Anthony of the Desert (251-356 A.D.). The desert became for them a wondrous and lifegiving milieu. Their reasons for being there were varied. For the earlier hermits, the desert was often an escape from persecution and a place to seek holiness through asceticism. For many of the fiercely independent Egyptian peasants, the desert was a route of escape from insurmountable economic burdens. For yet others, the flight from the new Christian cities was a protest against the church turned too worldly and over-institutionalized, now that it was established in the Empire and no longer persecuted. The desert became the locus for austere alternate lifestyles. Later in the first age of religious

life, the flight into the desert was related to the expectation of the end of
the world as threatened by the imminence of the so-called barbarian invasions.

Whatever the motivation, these lay men and women were inspired by
the image of the holy ascetic who seeks Christ in the "desert," living in
solitary or in community with a group of hermits (cenobites) under the
care and guidance of a master ascetic. In the footsteps of Christ, they
fought the devil through prayer and mortification and at times returned
to their fellow Christians who saw in the hermit the power to heal, com-
fort, challenge, reconcile and, above all, to remind them that nothing in
the world is more important than the love of Christ.

This movement began in the Egyptian desert and on the eastern rim
of the Mediterranean and gradually spread west to the Italian penin-
sula, Spain, Gaul, and the northern coast of Africa. It attracted men and
women from all strata of society. At first only embryonic communities
existed with no stable rule. Gradually some regulation was needed to
counter extravagant and delusionary ascetical practices like sitting on
pillars, loading oneself with chains, living on all fours, or deliberately
cultivating decay. Great cenobia (communities of hermits) with simple
rules were founded by people like Pachomius and Mary, Melania, Basil,
Augustine of Hippo and Cassian. The cenobia attracted thousands
of ascetics, even families. Perhaps ten thousand ascetics were network-
ed in Egypt by Pachomius and Mary alone.

The decline of the desert ideal occurred as the Roman Empire
weakened under the barbarian onslaught and as ties between the eastern and western halves of the Empire began to break apart. The cenobia were not without their own problems. Some cenobia became em-
broiled in doctrinal controversy; others were debilitated by pederasty;
yet others became cloisters for those fleeing the barbarians.

But, even as the western Roman Empire collapsed, Brigit was founding the monastery of Kildare (480 A.D.). A new ideal, that of monasticism, was taking root in Ireland.

The Age of Monasticism (500-1200 A.D.)

With the collapse of the western half of the Roman Empire under the barbarian invasions, Europe was thrown into the Dark Ages. The countryside was unstable, western civilization as it was known was in decline, and chaos reigned. It was in this milieu that a new dominant image of religious life took shape: to live as a monk or a nun in a monastery according to a holy rule under the guidance of an abbot or abbess. Life in community became an element as essential as the solitary life had been previously.

There are many great names associated with monasticism; but the greatest for the church in the West is undoubtedly Benedict. Benedict was a hermit and probably a layman; not a very successful hermit perhaps, because his solitude was disturbed by many followers who sought his constant guidance. In 529 A.D. he assembled a few of them and founded the monastery at Monte Cassino (Italy), and wrote for them the famous RULE, which, because of its wisdom and simplicity and flexibility, became a basic model of religious life even to our own day. The RULE contained both a vision of the basic principles of religious life and a structure for a communal life of prayer and labor within the monastery. As circumstances changed and the needs of the church became more manifest, the RULE also provided for apostolic activity both within and outside the monastery. Monks sometimes engaged in both educational and missionary activity.

The enormous influence of Benedict and the numbers of people involved in monastic life can be inferred by the fact that in the eleventh century the federation gathered around the foundation of Cluny in Burgundy numbered over one thousand monasteries.

However, Benedict's was not the only rule. Many rules existed both before and after Benedict. Some seventy-five years before the founding of Monte Cassino, other rules were already being observed in Irish monasteries. Unhampered by the collapse of the rest of Europe, Ireland experienced a vigorous growth of monastic life from the sixth century well into the golden age of Celtic monasticism in the eighth century. Benedict's RULE became the norm eventually, but not until Celtic (along with Anglo-Saxon) monasticism made its mark. The Irish are the ones to be credited for being the main carriers of Christianity from the final days of the Roman Empire to the founding centuries of Christendom in the early Middle Ages. Some Irish monks even became missionaries, founding numerous monasteries all over Europe. The Irish church itself was transformed by monasticism. It became an organization centered less around dioceses and bishops than around monasteries and abbots.

One should not get the impression that monasticism was under the exclusive control of men. Women had their own monasteries, shared "double monasteries" with men, and at times even had the upper hand. From 1100 A.D. to the French Revolution, for example, the monastery of Fontevrault was home to both monks and nuns living under the rule of one single major superior. That single major superior was always for all those centuries a woman.[2]

Monasticism also incorporated lay persons. Fontevrault, for example, included lay sisters; and Rievaulx, the Cistercian monastery, some 600 lay brothers. These lay people were given a home in the monastery, a daily schedule and a juridic status of "lay brothers not monks." They were people from a class which had previously been excluded from monastic life, the laborers and free peasants. In an age of rising population, thousands responded to the call to work with the monks and nuns, cultivating the land, creating new settlements, and maintaining the monasteries. The work of the brothers and sisters freed the monks and nuns for more prayer and study than their usual workload allowed.[3]

Monasticism like all forms of religious life eventually experienced a decline. Internally, some monasteries became wealthy and lax. Reforms were called for and reformist models of monastic life emerged, such as the Carthusians and the Cistercians. Petty contentions erupted over the superiority of celibacy over married life and of priesthood over the lay state. Externally, society at the end of the twelfth century was experiencing the first stirrings of urbanization with the growth of medieval towns. Monastic rules adequate for the feudal culture of the Dark Ages were not adequate in the face of the beginnings of world trade and contact with the Arab civilization which occasioned the recovery of antiquity.

A new ideal of Christian life was emerging which contrasted sharply with monasticism.[4] Under the monastic ideal, living the apostolic life of the Gospel was equated with being a monk or a nun. The Christian was the monk or nun. Lay people could participate by becoming lay brothers and sisters or by associating themselves in some way to the monastery. The closer one's association with the monastery, the more Christian one's life. The monastery was the city of God into which all society was to be led—an apt image for a feudal society.

With the breakdown of the feudal system came the new ideal of Christian life. The privileged beneficiaries were no longer the monks but the poor ones at the edge of feudal society, the merchants. To live as the early Christians did, one did not have to be a professed monk, pray the canonical office or live the rule in a monastery. One only had to renounce the "world", be baptized and live out one's calling or state of life evangelizing the world. Only one rule was necessary, the rule of the Gospel. It mattered not whether one prayed the canonical office, only that one prayed—and many forms of prayer became popular: chaplets, rosaries, celebrations of the joyful mysteries of Mary's life, as well as some contemplative observances. The locus of Christian living shifted from the rural monasteries to the towns and cities. The church was to be planted in the world, present to the world, evangelizing the world and testifying to its errors.

The Age of the Mendicant Orders (1200-1500 A.D.)

The Dominicans and the Franciscans were among the many orders of men and women whose foundation accompanied the growth of the medieval towns. Along with the new ideal of Christian life in general came the new ideal of "religious life": the holy beggar or mendicant who eschewed the landed wealth of the monastery to live evangelical poverty in the streets, preaching and teaching at the service of the church wherever needed.

The mendicants belonged to a community of houses called a "province." Unlike monks and nuns bound by stability to one house, they were easily sent to many. The contrast of mendicant life with life inside the monasteries was so sharp that the mendicants were often confused with the heretical groups of the time. While monastic life stood for stability, contemplation and security in rural retreats, mendicant life professed mobility, apostolate and begging in urban centers.

The 12th and 13th centuries saw a rapid development of lay piety and a corresponding effort at bonding between the mendicant orders and the laity.[5] Convinced that all men and women are children of God created for love and service, Francis of Assisi invited all, including married persons and clerics, to adopt a lifestyle of conversion which came to be known as "the penance." The rule of 1228 specified this lifestyle. Members of the "order of penitents," for example, were to dress simply, fast frequently, pray the divine office, refuse to bear arms, gather monthly into separate fraternities and sororities to hear Mass and listen to instruction and spiritual direction from a male religious, engage in works of charity, pray for the dead and attend funerals of their deceased members. Dissension was to be settled peaceably. Each fraternity or sorority was to be visited regularly by a delegate of the bishop who would critique it for its shortcomings in lifestyle and prescribe punishment or dispensation.

Why would ordinary persons make such a demanding public commitment to penance? Several factors were involved. One was the spirit of the times, as expressed in the new ideal of Christian life mentioned above. A new religious climate was developing in the later half of the 12th century, especially in the towns of northern Italy and the valleys of the Rhine and the Rhone, which were among the first to profit from the new wealth and trade and the first to expand the weaving industry. Distrusting sacerdotalism and sacramentalism, people longed to return to the Scriptures, read them in their own language, imitate the early apostolic communities, gather in associations, meet for prayer, live simply and organize for charity. The ministry of the local clergy did not satisfy this thirst.

> The rift, especially in Italy and Provence, between the official, moneyed Church, whether of high ecclesiastics or great religious corporations, and the masses of the people, whether well-to-do townspeople or illiterate peasantry, was yearly growing wider, and the threats to the sacerdotal and sacramental system foreshadowed a cleavage such as did in fact take place three hundred years later.[6]

Lay people looked beyond the official church and found rules of life that had been popularized by Francis and given body espescially by Dominic, founder of the Dominican Friars. Francis and Dominic had seen the danger of a popular piety detached from the pastors of the church and they initiated rules of life that encouraged obedience to the bishop under the guidance of a religious.

Another factor which contributed to the rise of the penitential orders was the popular understanding of penance. Given the decline in sacramental penance and penitential practices in our own century, the medieval attraction to penance as a lifestyle may seem strange. But, in a time marked by the possibility of sudden death from war, plague and unexplained natural disasters, people feared the pains of hell that might befall the unrepentant sinner. They wished to be forgiven by sacramental confession and relieved of temporal punishment due to sin through prayer, fasting and almsgiving. The order of penitents provided people with a means to live a converted and repentant lifestyle without entering the monastery or cloister.

The relationship between the friars and the penitents was mutually beneficial. Together they sponsored charitable works. The penitents provided the needed social and financial foundations; and the friars, the pastoral care of the clients and the spiritual formation, direction and guidance of the penitents.

The relationship was not without its tensions. The penitents experienced a decline in fervor around the end of the 13th century. Friars were expected to negotiate if penitents were in trouble or in financial debt. The friars resented the pastoral care of penitents when it infringed upon their liberty to do their ordinary pastoral work like preaching. The friars themselves were often resented by the secular clergy because of the privileges accorded them. Economic control of the public charitable works by the penitents became controversial among penitent groups as well as between penitents and friars.

In the late 13th century another rule appeared which reorganized and tightened the structure of the penitential life and added elements that gave it a particularly Dominican flavor. The spirit of Francis and this later rule of the Sisters and Brothers of Penance of Blessed Dominic emerged as the model for other orders of penitents of the 14th and 15th centuries.

While the 13th century brought rapid expansion of the mendicant orders (the Dominicans alone grew to thirteen thousand in just forty years), the 14th century brought flagrant laxity among both monks and mendicants. The Black Death in 1349 took a heavy toll among those who generously nursed the sick and dying, so that the Reformers to come were often quite justified in their complaints about the less than generous religious that remained.

The Age of the Apostolic Orders (1500-1800 A.D.)

Spectacular changes occurred in Europe at the onset of the 16th century. The Renaissance delved deeply into antiquity, while the discovery of the New World and the printing press opened horizons into the future. The enthusiasm over new possibilities for European society contrasted sharply with the popular disrespect toward the Church and religious life.

The Reformation, sparked by Luther in 1517, obliterated religious life in Protestant Europe. But in Catholic Europe a new ideal of religious life took shape. As modeled by the Ursulines (1535) and the Jesuits (1540), the new religious life was an elite corps of men and women dedicated to the new needs of the Counter-Reformation Church. Their apostolic service consisted of intellectual pursuit, instruction, the implementation of Trent, Church diplomacy, charitable works and foreign mission. Their service was to be rooted in a disciplined life of personal prayer and meditation. But these religious valued mobility, detachment and availability over traditional characteristics of religious life such as lifelong residence in one monastery, decision-making by individual communities in Chapter, choice of superiors by the individual communities, and the daily chanting of Holy Office in choir.

Involvement in the apostolate as a primary goal for religious was a radical concept at the time, particularly for women religious. The Council of Trent and the Vatican could hardly conceive of women living religiously outside of the cloister. The Ursulines in the Paris foundation were pressured into cloister; but the original Ursulines lived in their homes and, much like the secular institute members of today, formed a loose-knit company of virgins devoted to assisting the poor and caring for the sick. In the course of the seventeenth and eighteenth centuries, however, women found ways of being apostolic without the cloister. Some orders, like the Daughters of Charity and the Sisters of St. Joseph, insisted that they were not "religious" and so escaped the Tridentine requirement of cloister and freely pursued their active apostolates.

The French Revolution marked the decline of the apostolic orders. The orders of men, for instance, included 300,000 before the Revolution, the majority of these being mendicants; after, 70,000 remained. Many orders closed down or were suppressed by the state or by Rome, as the Jesuits were in 1773. The Enlightenment took its toll as well. Rationalism undermined the existence of religious life not to mention that of the church as a whole.

The Age of the Teaching Congregations (1800 A.D.-present)

Religious life was not dead as some pessimists predicted at the end of the eighteenth century. In fact, about 600 new communities were founded during the industrial revolution of the nineteenth century. Democracy was on the rise and the largest immigration of peoples in fifteen centuries was taking place. A new religious ideal emerged: caring for the masses of people by creating and professionally staffing institutions like hospitals and schools. The pursuit of holiness became identified with humble dedication to a community's institutions. Whereas earlier religious institutes had often aimed at christianizing the elite, the congregations recognized the power of institutions to christianize the masses. Religious now conceived of themselves as special auxiliaries to the bishops, doing what the ordinary clergy could not do. Women religious, gradually liberated from the requirement of cloister, now emerged as key actors in the apostolate of institutions.

At the time of the Second Vatican Council, membership of religious institutes had reached its zenith. Never before in history were the institutes so large, their institutions so numerous, or their governments so centralized. Centralization under the authority of Rome had become a distinctive mark of religious institutes, as of the whole church since the French Revolution. Many institutes established headquarters in Rome and centralized their decision-making there. Hence from Rome came the 1917 Code of Canon Law with rulings on religious life as well as an unprecedented number of documents specifically on religious life.[7]

The American Experience

Since the Second Vatican Council, religious life has experienced its first major decline in a century and a half. The winds of the Council and major changes in world societies seem to be suggesting a new course for religious life.

The church in the U.S. has experienced only one of the five ages of religious life. It is no wonder that the present crisis of religious life is creating shock, disillusionment and fear. Never before has the U.S. church directly experienced a transition time between one age and another.

Religious life began to take hold in the U.S. only around 1830 during the age of the teaching congregations when tide after tide of immigrants began to arrive from Europe. Until that time the U.S. was very much a mission country. Religious order priests, especially Sulpicians, Dominicans and Augustinians, far outnumbered diocesan clergy. These European born and trained religious planted the seeds of the U.S. church and some became its first bishops. There were fewer women than men religious in this missionary church until around 1830 when both women and men religious flowed into the country following each successive tide of immigrants and the consequent elaboration of church structures.[8] From 1830 to 1900, approximately 220 religious communities established houses. Women's foundations outnumbered men's four to one.

As the immigrant church matured in the first half of the twentieth century, the congregations of men yielded diocesan sees and parishes to the local clergy and turned to preaching missions and retreats and educating men at secondary and higher levels. The women staffed charitable institutions, colleges for women, hospitals and parochial elementary and secondary schools. Other men and women religious pursued the contemplative life.

From 1900 to 1965 another 310 congregations established houses, with women's foundations once again outnumbering men's. By now, however, the great majority of religious were first and second generation immigrants.

About 65 percent of European-based communities who came to minister in the U.S. in the 19th century are no longer here. Seventy percent of the communities serving in the U.S. church today were founded by Americans in the early and middle 1800's.[9] Recent Official Catholic Directories report that the U.S. presently numbers about 413 religious institutes of women and 131 of men.[10]

By the end of World War II religious life in the U.S. had completely adapted itself to the needs of the immigrant church. It now began, with the rest of the church, to adapt to American society and culture. Three trends took on major significance:

(1) Religious heeded the call of Pope Pius XII in 1950 (General Conference on the State of Perfection, Rome) to return to the spirit or charisms of their founders and to adapt their customs to the needs of the times. Since Vatican II, religious have been rewriting their rules and constitutions and the church has published new canons on religious life.[11]

(2) Women religious organized themselves to take better advantage of educational opportunities. As recently as the 1950's, women religious were not admitted into the graduate theology programs in Catholic universities and seminaries. The Religious Formation Conference was founded to provide continuing education for sisters, and formation programs for young religious were reorganized.[12]

(3) When in the late 1950's the Pope urged Americans to send 10 percent of their personnel to the missions of South America, Asia and Africa, the congregations responded generously and began a flow of missionary personnel which, in return, re-enlivened the U.S. church's awareness of global realities and needs.

About the time of Vatican II, worldwide membership in religious communities had reached the highest point in the history of the church, surpassing even the maximums that had been achieved before the French Revolution. After the Council, however, the trend reversed itself for the first time in 150 years. Withdrawals increased and recruitment decreased. In the U.S., from 1966 to 1983, membership in women's communities declined 33 percent; in men's communities, 14 percent. More significantly perhaps, the number of student-candidates for communities of men and women declined somewhere between 82 percent and 86 percent.[13] According to the 1986 U.S. Catholic Directory, there are 113,658 sisters, 7,429 brothers and 22,028 religious priests in U.S. religious institutes.

A recent survey reports that the three major problems being faced internally by religious institutes are recruitment, the care of the elderly, and finances.[14] The three problems are closely connected. Since influx of new candidates is very low, the average age of religious is climbing steadily and the needs of the elderly are placing a severe strain on diminishing incomes.

Despite the severe problems, the adaptation of religious life to the needs of the times continues. While continuing their traditional works in the realm of direct care for the hungry, the sick, the ignorant, religious now give added attention to the causes of such poverty and to needed structural reform.[15] Their social mission is being reconceived and reorganized in terms of structural change.

When sisters speak of the work they want their congregations to do, 77 percent still put teaching as a top priority; 50 percent also want work with poor and homeless women; 55 percent, social service work of all kinds; 52 percent community development. In summary, 60 percent are ready for work that alleviates the results of poverty; 40 percent for work that eliminates its causes (Sisters' Survey, 1980).[16]

The traditional work of the "teaching congregations" through institutions is also being rethought. Institutions which once served the immigrant church so well may not be appropriate to today's needs or may require transformation. As the sociologist Sister Marie Augusta Neal states so well...

People do not join religious institutes to fulfill corporate goals within profit-making systems. They just do the work that Jesus did and, if that does not exist within the institute, they stop coming.[17]

Shapes of the Future

A number of generalizations can be drawn from this quick overview of the history of religious life and of bonding between religious and laity:

(1) Religious community life in the church is certainly not a static, unchanging institution. On the contrary, it has evolved through several stages and transitions, periods of growth, stability and decline, as well as death.[18]

(2) Religious community life has taken on new forms in response to major changes in history. As one of the most thorough studies of the matter indicates,

...major turning points are likely to occur in religious life when both the Church and secular culture are in the midst of major changes and when religious life itself is disoriented by upheaval.[19]

(3) Religious community life is probably experiencing such a turning point in response to changes in both the church and society. The church after Vatican II is shifting in at least three ways: toward ecumenism away from Counter-Reformation; toward greater rapprochement with non-Christian religions; and toward relating with a secular world no longer perceived as enemy. U.S. society is shifting as well toward what some commentators call a post-Modern Era which will at least be post-Christian, post-humanist, post-industrial, post-competitive, and post-materialist.[20]

(4) The forms of the future are perhaps already taking shape in several contemporary movements: the rise of secular institutes, the feminist consciousness among Christian women including women religious, the hidden apostolates of the Little Brothers and Sisters of Jesus and the "worker priests," the "non-canonical communities," the ecumenical community at Taize in France, the Charismatic communities, and the worldwide growth of intentional Christian communities. Chapter Four of this book explores a few of these futuristic forms.

If indeed ours is a time of transition for "religious life" and for Christian life as a whole and if such transition demands a fresh new look at the needs of the world, the church will once again look to the laity for insight and spiritual energy. In the words of historian and theologian M.-D. Chenu,

It is consistently true that when the church, in circumstances like these, seeks to find again its proper theatre of activity in the world, it has recourse to laymen [sic], who are familiar with and inhabit this world, and not first to clerics, who have more or less abandoned it.[21]

Discussion Questions

1. Is there a history of lay-religious collaboration in the religious community with which you are associated? What is your personal experience of that history?

2. What historical factors most affect your own experience of bonding between laity and religious?

3. Is the transition presently being experienced by religious life in the U.S.A. actually happening to you and your religious community in your particular situation? How is your experience similar/ dissimilar to that described in this chapter?

4. To which of the historical transitions of religious life is the present transition most similar? Most dissimilar? How?

Footnotes

1. This author is deeply indebted to the work of Lawrence Cada, Raymond Fitz, Gertrude Foley, Thomas Giardino and Carol Lichtenberg. Their book SHAPING THE COMING AGE OF RELIGIOUS LIFE (Whitinsville, MA: Affirmation Books, 1979, pb, 196pp.) is a groundbreaking study of the history and present transition of religious life. I have relied heavily on their categories, while trying to elaborate the more specific history of lay/religious bonding. Gratitude is also due to the researcher on whom these writers based their own work: Raymond Hostie, Vie Et Mort Des Ordres Religieux. Paris: Desclee, 1972. Translation: Life and Death of Religious Orders. Washington, D.C.: Center for Research in the Apostolate, 1983 (a very limited printing and not widely available).

2. David Knowles, FROM PACHOMIUS TO IGNATIUS: A STUDY IN THE CONSTITUTIONAL HISTORY OF RELIGIOUS ORDERS (London: Clarendon Press Oxford, 1966, 98pp.), p. 34. This book focuses on the stage by stage development of the fully articulated and integrated religious order.

3. Knowles supposes that the original intention that the monks should live by the work of their own hands had soon proved unworkable. The lay brothers and sisters provided an economic alternative. See pp. 29-30.

4. M.-D. Chenu, O.P., NATURE, MAN AND SOCIETY IN THE TWELFTH CENTURY. Chicago: University of Chicago Press, 1968, 361pp. See especially chapters 6 and 7. See also R. W. Southern, WESTERN SOCIETY AND THE CHURCH IN THE MIDDLE AGES (The Pelican History of the Church: 2) Penguin Books, England, 1970, pb, 376 pp.

5. Thomas J. Johnston, O.P., "Franciscan and Dominican Influences on the Medieval Order of Penance: Origins of the Dominican Laity," SPIRITUALITY TODAY, vol. 37 no. 2, summer 1985, pp.108-119. In the same issue of the journal, also see Donna Marie F. Kaminski, "Secular Franciscans: Bearers of Peace, Messengers of Joy," pp. 120-129.

6. Knowles, p. 34.

7. John W. Padburg, "Memory, Vision and Structure: Historical Perspectives on the Experience of Religious Life in the Church," RELIGIOUS LIFE IN THE U.S. CHURCH: THE NEW DIALOGUE, Robert J. Daly, S.J. (Ed.) and others (N.Y.: Paulist Press, 1984, 345pp.), p.76. The volume contains especially helpful articles by Gray, Flaherty, Kennelly, Neal, and Donovan.

8. Women religious, however, had made significant inroads, as James Hennesey reports: "In colonial times a number of Maryland women had joined contemplative monasteries in the Low Countries and France. Driven out by the French Revolution, three of them, with Mother Bernardine Matthews as superior, were among the founders of a Carmel at Port Tobacco, Maryland, in 1790. Ursulines, in New Orleans since 1727, attempted schools in New York City (1812-15) and Boston (1820-34). Visitandines were at Georgetown." Hennesey continues listing other early ventures. See James Hennessey, S.J., AMERICAN CATHOLICS: A HISTORY OF THE ROMAN CATHOLIC COMMUNITY IN THE UNITED STATES. N.Y.: Oxford University Press, 1981, p. 92.

9. Helen Flaherty, "Religious Life in the U.S.—A Guess at the Future," RELIGIOUS LIFE IN THE U.S. CHURCH, p. 297.

10. Figures about religious groups are misleading. While it is accurate to say that there are about 413 religious institutes of women and 131 of men, it is also true, as was stated in a footnote in Chapter One, that there are about 600 autonomous communities of women and about 300 of men. The discrepancy between the two sets of figures is due to the fact that several "autonomous communities" may belong to the same "religious institute" (e.g., the Adrian Dominican Sisters belong to the Dominican family and carry the initials "O.P." after their names).

11. According to the 1982 Code of Canon Law there are two types of religious groups: institutes of consecrated life and societies of apostolic life.

The institutes of consecrated life include both religious institutes and secular institutes. Jesuits, Franciscans (both men and women), Oblates of Mary Immaculate are "religious institutes" as are monastic orders such as the Benedictines, the Cistercians and the Carmelites. Groups like the Missionaries of the Kingship of Christ, the Oblate Missionaries of Mary Immaculate, and the Teresian Institute are among those called "secular institutes." Religious institutes are those "in which members, according to proper law, pronounce public vows and lead a community life in common." Secular institutes, on the other hand, are those "in which Christians living in the world, seek the perfection of charity, and work for the sanctification of the world, especially from within." The members of these institutes, both religious and secular, lead a life which is said to be consecrated to God by a "new and special title" effected by profession of the evangelical counsels of chastity, poverty, and obedience. Hermits and consecrated virgins are also considered as living "consecrated life."

The second major category of institutes are the "societies of apostolic life." Counted among these are the Congregation of the Most Precious Blood, the Society of the Catholic Apostolate (Pallottines), and the Society of Missionary Priests of St. Paul the Apostle (Paulists). These are similar to institutes of consecrated life, but their members pursue, without religious vows, an apostolic end and lead a community life in common. According to their own mode, they seek the perfection of charity through the observance of constitutions. In some societies, the evangelical counsels are assumed by a bond prescribed in the constitutions. The title and name given to these societies indicate that their nature, end, manner of life and spirituality are characterized by a dedication to an apostolate within the mission of the whole church.

There are two other traditional forms of consecrated life which are now recognized in Canon Law: the Hermits and the Virgins. The Hermits are an ancient tradition recently revived in the church. These men and women take vows or some other form of sacred bond, dedicate their lives to prayer and solitude, offer spiritual guidance and counsel to those who seek it from them, and they lead their lives under the guidance of the local bishop. Some religious institutes provide hermitages for their members (Canon 603).

Virgins are people who chose to live a life of consecrated celibacy and are so recognized by their bishops. They may or may not live in community or at their own homes (Canon 604).

In recent years a number of religious groups have asked the church to dispense them of their vows and allow them to assume a non-canonical status. Among these are the Immaculate Heart Community of Los Angeles which numbers about 300 and the Sisters for Christian Community which numbers about 700 and recruits former members of other religious groups.

Yet another category of church associations is the "personal prelature." Opus Dei is to date the only one in existence. Vatican II explains that personal prelatures exist "to facilitate specific pastoral activities with different social groups in some regions or nations, or indeed world-wide" (Decree Presbyterorum Ordinis, n. 10). For specific legislation, see Motu Proprio Ecclesiae Sanctae, I, n. 4. Until 1983, Opus Dei was recognized as a secular institute.

Types of Religious Groups

Institutes of Consecrated Life
Religious Institutes
o monastic
o apostolic
Societies of Apostolic Life
Hermits and Virgins
Secular Institutes

----

12. Marie Augusta Neal, "Who They Are and What They Do: Current Forms of Religious Life in the U.S. Church," in RELIGIOUS LIFE IN THE U.S. CHURCH, p.165.

13. Neal, p.162.

14. Neal, p. 167.

15. There are in the U.S. new poor and refugees who need direct care as well as structural reform. In the year 2000, the U.S. church could possibly be 45 percent Hispanic and 23 percent Asian.

16. Neal, p.164. Neal also notes that the number of sisters teaching declined 68 per cent from 1966 to 1983.

17. Neal, p.164-165.

18. Cada elaborates three characteristics which ease communities through critical periods of transition: "At least three characteristics can be singled out in all communities which have been revitalized in this way: a transforming response to the signs of the times; a reappropriation of the founding charism; and a profound renewal of the life of prayer, faith, and centeredness in Christ." p.60.

19. Cada, p.47.

20. Cada, p.50. For more extensive commentary, see Joe Holland and Peter Henriot, SOCIAL ANALYSIS, ORBIS PRESS and CENTER OF CONCERN, 1985. See also Helen Flaherty "Five Megatrends of Religious Life," RELIGIOUS LIFE IN THE U.S. CHURCH , p.299-300.

21. M.-D. Chenu, p. 220.

3

A Tradition Revived: Life As Religious

A regathering of the church is taking place. In response to and as a result of major historical and theological quakes, laity, religious and clergy are being regrounded and remobilized: regrounded in the sense that attention is being directed anew to shared common ground; and remobilized in that energies are being applied to new tasks.

The basic historical shift in the U.S. church involves the rise of post-immigrant Catholicism. The structures of the church which were designed specifically to serve immigrant catholics are developing major structural cracks. Among the most obvious systemic cracks is the severe decline in religious order membership and the consequent closing of traditional institutions and ministries. Schools, colleges, seminaries and ethnic parishes are in jeopardy, as are ministries once staffed by religious, like religious education. Many of the remaining members of the religious institutes are more interested in Kingdom-ministries (doing what Jesus did), both within relevant institutions and without, than in maintaining institutions for institutions' sake.[1] The religious working in institutions and ministries once responsive to the needs of the immigrant church are rethinking their mission.

When history shifts, so do pastoral questions. The strategic pastoral question which informs the allocation of church resources is no longer how to nurture and protect the faith of Catholic immigrants while helping them to integrate into American culture. The more appropriate question now perhaps is how to respect the positive elements in the culture of upwardly mobile American Catholics while nurturing and strengthening their faith so that it can impact a society and culture which has great potential for good but is in the same instance hostile to Christian values.

The shift in strategic questions requires a rethinking of pastoral ministries and a reorganization of energies. The mission of the church in society is being questioned and hence so are the ministries which serve that mission. Some of the structures of mission and ministry are toppling. Rebuilding is needed, but on the solid ground of baptismal call and commitment and in loving response to new needs. There is no sense in rebuilding a devastated city on severely damaged or unstable land. Nor is there sense in repairing buildings which are too weak to survive another quake or which were too inadequate to truly serve human needs even before the quake.

The Second Vatican Council was part of a quake which affected not only the U.S. church but the world church as well. From the Council emerged a People of God understanding of church which regathered the faithful on the common ground of baptism. This ecclesiology stresses that all of the People share a common call to holiness, mission and ministry; that the gifts and functions of the members serve the community and the mission; and that the mission is directed to persons and the society of which they are part.

Regrouping around new historical mission implies some blurring and redistribution of responsibilities, roles, lines of communication, and group boundaries. It involves a reinterpretation of history from a new perspective. Within the church, regrouping gives new importance to the discernment of spirits. Old questions return seeking new answers: How is the spirit of prophecy moving today?—that same spirit which inspired the religious community life movement throughout the centuries. How is the spirit of priesthood moving?—that same spirit which has shaped the pastoral life of the church since its foundation? How is the Spirit shaping and challenging the church today?

The regathering of church is happening in many places. One is where the new patterns of bonding are developing between religious and laity. These two distinct groups within the church are exploring anew their common faith and finding in each other the resources of a prophetic tradition and sensitivity to the needs of people and communities in a changing culture. The boundaries between religious and laity are being blurred by a new spirit of mission and holiness. Some believe that this blurring is an identity crisis which can be resolved by simply reinforcing traditional identities. Others believe it to be a major step toward a more wholesome integration of calls and gifts which had been artificially separated. In either case, the bonding of religious and laity is providing the space in which to discern the movements of the Spirit which have caused such disruption and questioning.

The aim of this chapter is to develop a set of criteria by which to plan and evaluate collaborative efforts between laity and religious. The criteria are derived from two sources, one theological and pastoral, and the other historical and cultural.

In respect to the first, this chapter describes the new self-concepts emerging among laity and religious within the context of the Second Vatican Council. Then, in respect to the second, it explores the changing historical circumstances which have occasioned new religious responses to U.S. culture and society.

Such criteria are useful to laity and religious in a variety of circumstances: when planning volunteer, associate or co-worker efforts; when evaluating such collaboration; when praying or reflecting on common mission; when attempting to resolve a problem which has arisen in a collaborative relationship; or when discerning new calls, new forms of common life and shared mission.[2] These criteria describe, in terms consistent with Vatican II and the U.S. Bishops' reading of the signs of the times, the type of collaboration which laity and religious wish to foster with each other.

Vatican II

It has become a truism to speak of the emergence of the laity since the Second Vatican Council. But there is certainly no doubt that the self-identity of the Catholic layperson has shifted dramatically. Vatican II erupted on the hierarchical landscape of the Tridentine church with a fresh "People of God" ecclesiology which recognized the dignity and respect due to all the baptized, regardless of role or function.

There emerged from this shake-up new lay energies both for participation in ministry and decision-making within the church and for mission and evangelism in society. These energies have been channeled into movements like Cursillo, Marriage Encounter, and Charismatic Renewal; into parish programs like RENEW and Christ Renews His Parish; into the development of the Christian Initiation of Adults; and into the growth of Secular Institutes and Intentional Christian Communities.

Vatican II shifted the notion of laity predominant in the Catholic church since the Council of Trent in 1534. Chart V summarizes the shift in terms of the laity's call to holiness, mission and ministry.

Holiness

Those of us who are older than forty were clearly schooled in Trent's concept of the laity, especially if as children we were given the impression that we should all go study to be brothers, nuns and priests. It seemed as if God would be more pleased with that choice than with any other, not excluding marriage; but "better marry than burn." Pursuing a career was good, but better to "give one's life to God."

The Council of Trent proposed that the person seeking perfection should choose the higher way, the superior way of priesthood or religious life. The lay life was considered a sub-state of perfection.

Vatican II, on the other hand, recognized that all Christians, laity, religious and clergy alike, are called to holiness.

Chart V
The Role of the Laity

Vatican II

The baptized are called to holiness, mission and ministry.

Trent

The holiness of laity is a substate of perfection. Their mission is derived and compromised. Their ministry is to be "Father's helpers."

Mission

Trent conceived the mission of the church to society in terms of gathering people into the church, the "Bark of Peter." To be religious is to be separated from the sinful world and safely cloistered in the church. Laity are those whose participation in the mission is compromised, since they live in both the world and the church.

Vatican II recognized that the baptized are indeed in the world and that our mission is to the world. The faithful share the hopes and joys, griefs and anxieties of the people of the age, especially the poor and the afflicted.[3] The mission of all the baptized is to hasten the coming of the Kingdom, the Reign of God over all of creation.

Ministry

Trent understood the ministry of the church to the members of the church as the exclusive domain of the clergy. To them was reserved the "care of souls" in the name of the local bishop. Religious who were not ordained clergy, like laity, were to be "Father's helpers." Their call to ministry was conceived as deriving exclusively from his.

Vatican II recognized that ministry, like mission and holiness, is the calling not only of the clergy through ordination but of all the faithful through baptism. The baptized are entrusted to the pastoral care of the entire community. All are given gifts and talents for the good of the church and the pursuit of its mission.

***

The shift in the church's self-understanding from Trent to Vatican II has a number of implications for the shape of lay-religious bonding:

I
Language Problems

The shift from Trent to Vatican II led to a severe breakdown in the language of "laity" and "religious." The new People of God ecclesiology has turned those terms upside down so that one can say that laity are called to be "religious" (read: to be holy) and that religious are in the first instance "laity." To say that religious have a monopoly on being religious is inconsistent with the Council; for laity too have a baptismal vocation to holiness, ministry and mission. It is likewise inconsistent to say that laity have a monopoly on being the People of God. The very word "laity" is derived from the Greek word laos meaning "people." Religious too are part of the laos, as are clergy. Clergy and religious are first people of God and secondarily, servants of that People.

A similar language problem arises when we speak of "religious life" or "religious communities." We who are familiar with church-talk know that these terms commonly refer to religious institutes and societies. But, are not parishes and other gatherings, like Charismatic Renewal groups, also communities that are religious? Do they not also strive to live religious lives?

How then are we to speak of ourselves as religious or laity when our language excludes so much of the meaning we intend to include?

Effective lay-religious collaboration fosters, on an equal basis, the holiness, mission and ministry of all the baptized regardless of lifestyle or function.

II
Lay Founders

Inaccurate language can yield unfortunate results. Among these is the false impression that laity do not found institutes of consecrated life.

Many communities have in fact been founded by laypersons for laypersons. Benedict, Francis, and Briget were all lay. Many communities were never and still are not clerical. It was only after the 11th century that it became fashionable for male members to seek ordination.[4] After that some institutes were founded specifically as clerical institutes, but clerics certainly have had no monopoly on religious institutes. Nor have "nuns" or cloistered women. Many lay women founders were forced into cloister, especially before the Age of the Teaching Congregations. Some, however, successfully fought the traditional requirement of cloister by insisting that they were not solemnly vowed religious and that their mission was apostolic and not contemplative in nature.[5]

The bottom line is this: if lay persons founded religious communities then, why not now? The Spirit can and does indeed energize all kinds of people of God (lay, religious and clergy) to re-gather the faithful around new forms of community and paths to holiness. The founding of "institutes" and "societies," as Canon Law calls them, is no prerogative of clerics or religious.

The Spirit moves at will and in response to the needs of the times and the cries of the abandoned. The one whom the Spirit touches may be an unlikely character like the hermit Benedict (the Benedictines), the rich boy Francis (the Franciscans), Elizabeth Ann Seton who was the mother of several children (the Daughters of Charity), and Catherine Bostick who had been expelled from the Poor Clares because of chronic illness (the Eucharistic Missionaries of St. Dominic).

The Code of Canon Law recognizes explicitly the creativity of lay people with special vocations by reaffirming the vocation of hermits and virgins and by encouraging not only new institutes but new forms of consecrated life as well.[6] In our own times, will Christians be inspired to new forms of consecrated life? Will Christians be re-gathered around new ways to pursue holiness? Will new apostolates arise in response to the spiritual and temporal needs of society? Will those stranded at the edges of church or society once again be recognized and welcomed and embraced?

Effective lay-religious collaboration fosters an opennness to the Spirit which re-creates traditional religious communities and creates anew prophetic communities responsive to the signs of the times.

III
Lay Spirituality

A language breakdown is also evident in discussions about "lay spirituality." The phrase is used to refer to the kind of spirituality which is needed to support faith in the workplace, the marketplace, the civic arena, within the family, and in sexual relationships.[7] "Lay spirituality" is often contrasted with "monastic spirituality," which is said to hold sway in the church. Some members of religious institutes are rightly offended by the phrase because they too conceive of themselves as living "in the world" (not "out of this world"!) and sense the need for a spirituality which relates them positively to the world in which they have a mission.[8] The language of "lay spirituality" boxes its users into a pre-Council notion of religious life and emphasizes the differences in lifestyle that exist among the People of God.

That being said, however, the language of "lay spirituality" may be useful after all. Perhaps it can generate a spirituality that is more responsive to the experiences of a class of people (laity) who are only recently assuming equality and being heard in the church.[9] As one layman wrote in response to our survey, bonding efforts need to defend and protect the new "lay spirituality":

Prior to any type of bonding, the laity need to clarify and strengthen their identity. It is my sense that lay spirituality is not yet fully articulated enough to stand in the type of dialogue with a monastic spirituality necessary for bonding. I am also

concerned that bonding efforts between well-organized
religious orders and loosely or unorganized lay folks would
result in a loss of characteristics that are unique to the lay lifestyle. If bonding will facilitate the clarification and strengthening of a lay spirituality and lifestyle then perhaps that is the way
for us to move. However, I would move with caution.[10]

*Effective lay-religious collaboration fosters a spirituality which relates
positively to contemporary experiences of family, work, leisure, marketplace and civic responsibility.*

IV
Laity Forming Religious

Members of religious institutes are usually aware of the fact that they
have a rich legacy of charisms and spiritualities to pass on to the laity.
They organize formation and education programs for their lay associates. But, an increasing number are also becoming aware that the laity
have something to teach them. Perhaps laity should organize "formation
programs" for religious! They could share their own insights about the
struggle to live Christian life at the front lines of society. To the extent
that religious life has sheltered some from the world, such lessons would
lend realism to discussions about spiritual ideals and the mission of the
church in the world.[11]

A lay woman and co-worker of the Sisters of Mercy states the challenge to religious in this way:

I am asking you, today, to speak for us so that we can speak
for ourselves. Speak for us at the parish level so our talent and
work may be recognized. Speak for us in church structures so
that our presence will be sought. Speak for us on issues. Tell
the church that family issues such as divorce, birth control, teen
pregnancy, child and spouse abuse, drug and alcohol abuse, ho-
mosexuality and abortion need to be discussed by the Catholic

Church. Tell the church that families need more than repri-
mands and 'thou shalt nots.' Instead of standing passively by
and reciting doctrine, the church needs to provide love, support and understanding if society is to work through these problems. Invite us to talk with you on these issues. Your method
of dialogue and reflection would help many families to deal
with these problems.[12]

V

Lay Ministry

Since the Council, parishes have experienced a dramatic increase of
lay participation in pastoral ministry. Catholics are becoming more ac-
cepting of each other's pastoral care in education, liturgy, hospital ministry, counseling, and in many other forms.

If religious life is considered a way of life and ministry superior to
that of the laity, the logically appropriate role of the laity is to lend financial, spiritual and social support to that higher state. But if the life
and ministry of the laity is considered as yet another differentiation of
the baptismal call, then the lay state deserves support from the religious
as well. This mutual support is characteristic of the new bonding between laity and religious. Laity once organized into guilds and associations for the support of religious. Such organizations were and continue
to be powerful promoters of foreign missions and other worthy endeavors. But now, religious too are organizing—to promote the work of
laity.

Examples abound: Religious priests organize parishes around the
principle of lay ministry or serve intentional Christian communities
founded on that very principle. Religious help provide needed training
for lay pastoral ministers. Some institutes give significant financial support to lay organizations (like the American Catholic Lay Network and
the Chicago Call to Action) and to organizations which promote laity
(like the Pallottine Institute for Lay Leadership and Research). And yet

other religious speak up for the laity in books, through   lectures and
courses, and in the decision-making bodies of the church to which laity
may not have access. Many religious institutes have publicly declared
lay leadership development a major priority.

Sometimes promoting laity means not getting in the way. One layman who responded to our survey bemoaned the fact that in his diocese
men and women religious have assumed total control over programs
like the R.C.I.A. (Christian Initiation), emergency housing, etc. The
powers-that-be in the diocese, he claims, trust the religious more than
the lay folk. Laity now have difficulty contributing to these efforts, especially when "the religious do not want or ask for any advice from the
laity." The issue he raises is complex, but his point seems valid. Religious can positively facilitate lay ministry by not taking over the work
that laity could otherwise do themselves.

A lay couple who worked and lived in a retreat house setting with
religious men for two years express hope for equality between laity and
religious:

> While working with the religious community, we felt accepted
> and loved; but we also felt that we were being taken advantage
> of. Our experience with them was unique and we would not
> take it back for all the money in the world; but we sometimes
> wonder if the religious view the laity as precious gifts to a com-
> munity rather than disposable commodities ("they [the laity]
> come and they go—so what?"). We believe that religious need
> to put themselves in the shoes of the laity and laity need to put
> themselves in the shoes of the religious. Only then will we ac-
> cept one another and begin to grow as a priestly people.[13]

VI
The Membership Issue

While the People of God notion of Vatican II grounds all of the faithful in a common baptism, it also recognizes the differences among them in lifestyle and function. Building upon that notion, the Code of Canon Law attempts to protect the integrity of both religious and laity, especially at a time when an unusual number of lay men and women are requesting that religious open the doors of their houses and share the dedicated lives of their membership with others who feel called to serve with them for a while. The religious institute, like any other organization, needs clear and unambiguous definitions of who is and is not a member, particularly in terms of important rights and responsibilities.

Religious life, of course, is not a static entity. It is a historical movement. The meaning and parameters of membership for one age of religious life is not necessarily the same for another. As new forms of membership and affiliation emerge, Canon Law itself is reformulated to reflect the lessons learned. Granted this evolutionary dynamic, the present Canon Law pertaining to membership crystalizes some of the most cherished lessons of the past and, in that manner, can contribute to effective lay-religious bonding today and stimulate the discovery of new forms.

A very enlightening article has already been written on the laws of the church that relate to lay associate programs of religious institutes. Rather than retrace that territory, we focus on the article's conclusions which are most pertinent to the question of membership.[14]

First, lay associates are not really "members" of the institute. They only come to live or work with the members for a limited period of time and with different levels of commitment and intensity. They have none of the rights or obligations of members. Technically, therefore, it is inappropriate and misleading to call them "members."

Second, canon law and community regulations seek to protect the common life appropriate to members who have made lifelong commitments to celibate chastity. But, the lifestyle of apostolic institutes and societies of the apostolic life is contingent upon the apostolic goals for which these institutes have been established. Some adaptation and accommodation can prudently be made in community life so as to foster apostolic work with the cooperation of lay men and women who are prepared to serve on a temporary basis. In the words of the author:

> In making these adjustments in lifestyle, there are a variety of important values to be considered; e.g., a community life that is appropriate and expected for those who have a celibate commitment; one that recognizes the real demands of the apostolate in which all are engaged; and, finally, a community life that can integrate laymen and women into it with the awareness of their particular needs, while recognizing the real benefits of such a cooperative venture for the good of the apostolate.

So, thirdly, it is important that goals and expectations, roles and responsibilities be carefully delineated from the beginning of the lay-religious relationship. Clarity in these matters helps obviate confusion, disorientation, discontentment and detrimental effects to the apostolate. Such agreements are most helpful if they are in writing.

Fourth, the author suggests that lay associates of a local house have some participation in the decision-making process when those decisions will also affect their lives and apostolate.

Finally, it is suggested, since not everyone is suited to either common life or to such a cooperative venture, that personnel and applicants be carefully selected and prepared and that the program be periodically evaluated.

The integrity of the lay lifestyle (single or married) needs to be respected as well. Just as the religious institute member has responsibility for the community and its apostolate, the lay person has responsibility for family, work and other commitments.

These responsibilities are primary and those of the bonding relationship are clearly secondary. Hence lay-religious bonding, as the phrase is used in this book, is not an effort at recruitment—either on the part of religious institute members or single lay persons! Inevitably, some will discern a calling to either the married life or the life of the religious institute and will indeed pursue that calling. But, the bonding relationship itself is built on the assumption that the respective responsibilities of laity and religious institute members will be respected.

Having so sharply defined the differences between laity and religious, however, Canon Law recognizes that new forms of religious community life will emerge and new categories may have to be created. The categories of "religious" and "lay" hardly suffice to explain new forms of community life like that of the "resident community" at Saint Benedict Center in Madison, WI.

Effective lay-religious collaboration recognizes that both laity and religious have primary responsibilities outside of their relationship, and that the integrity of their respective lifestyles needs to be respected.

The Signs of the Times

History and culture are a necessary source of criteria for collaborative relationships between laity and religious for three major reasons.

The first is that the evolution of religious life is in part a reaction and a response to particular social contexts. One of the most significant historical studies of religious life indicates that

...major turning points are likely to occur in religious life when both the Church and secular culture are in the midst of major changes and when religious life itself is disoriented by upheaval.[15] Since the age of the hermits and the early monks, each of the new shapes of religious life has come about in response or in reaction to such changes. The later half of the twentieth century is clearly a period of ecclesial as well as social upheaval. If the authors of the study are right, religious life is now undergoing a pervasive transition that will last for the next twenty to twenty-five years and will significantly change the life and service of religious communities.

The second reason is that the lifestyle of Christian laity also takes on new shapes under the influence of the social context. The change which came about in the 12th and 13th centuries is one of many examples. At that time, feudalism was collapsing and with it the ideal of monasticism and the identification of the ordinary Christian's life with the monastery. With the rise of the new cities built around the merchants came the new ideal of mendicant life and the notion of Christian living as a life of continual conversion to Gospel values, not in relation to the monastery but in the very streets of the cities. Today, in the U.S., Catholics who were once predominantly immigrants have become upwardly mobile. The ideal of Christian living which was appropriate for the immigrant no longer fits the majority. If the social milieu is indeed a major influence on the shape of religious life and of Christian living in general, then it would seem important that those of us involved in collaborative efforts between religious and laity be particularly sensitive to the changes in that milieu.

A third reason that history and culture are a necessary source of criteria for collaborative relationships is that faith shoulders a social responsibility. The social teachings of the church are emphatically clear: the church's mission of evangelization is not directed simply to oneself or to one's relationships with other individuals; it includes social, cultural, political and economic relations as well.[16] In the words of the 1971 Synod of Bishops:

> Action on behalf of justice and participation in the transformation of the world fully appear to us as a constitutive dimension of the preaching of the Gospel...[17]

Hence, faith impels the Christian on at least three levels: (1) to pray, grow in faith and care for one's self; (2) to care for others around us, like family, friends and neighbors, especially those most in need; and (3) to support the social structures in which we live when they respect human dignity, foster human rights and promote human development. Mature Christian faith is particularly sensitive to the cry of the poor and particularly responsive to social structures which create and maintain poverty.

Each of the stories at the beginning of the first chapter of this book illustrates how lay-religious collaboration can nurture Christian social responsibility. Gail's association with the Bon Secours sisters, for example, admittedly deepened her concern about justice issues such as the proper care of AIDS patients and the education of the public for more generous response to the victims. Through the weekly dialogues with the associates about the presence of God in their lives, Gail grew in awareness that her work at the hospital and with her family is her ministry, her work to hasten the Kingdom.

Arthur and Brenda and the Franciscans also show accountability to the social dimension of faith. They analysed their social situation and took action when it became clear that their Brazilian pastoral work would be irrelevant to the needs of the people unless the issue of land tenure was faced. Today they work closely with the Pastoral Land Commission sponsored by the Brazilian Bishops, who as a body have taken a strong position in favor of land reform.

Harold and the other members of the Missionary Cenacle Apostolates scan society for the most abandoned. In his words:

> Our apostolate is by design not in the mainstream institutional setting. We look for those who are not in the mainstream and whose needs are not met by the mainstream. We have to be careful not to be assimilated into mainstream structures. So, we who work with the abandoned often feel abandoned ourselves. But that is our unique mission.

All three of these examples show a sensitivity to faith's mission within the structures of society and to the evolving needs of the people who are abandoned by those structures. Their sensitivity is not unlike that of Francis and Dominic toward the merchants in feudal Europe or that of the founders of the teaching congregations toward the immigrants in our own country. Then and now, that sensitivity to the abandoned has gifted both religious and laity with spiritual growth and a new sense of mission.

Vatican II was a breakthrough for the awareness of the role of the church in the world, but it also marked the end of an era in the history of the U.S. Catholic Church. By the early 1960's Catholics who were once immigrants had grown significantly in social status, wealth, knowledge, influence and power. As their standing in society increased, vocations to priesthood declined, as did vocations to religious institutes, among them the "teaching congregations" which had channeled the energies of so many men and women toward the needs of the immigrant church. The needs of society and the needs of Catholics were changing. Today, the church, including the emerging laity and the religious communities in renewal, is still struggling to envision and create the structures to meet those needs.

The bishops of the U.S. have modeled a contemporary approach to Christian social responsibility. In pastoral letters addressed to Catholics and to the nation at large, they have set a social agenda for the faith and have begun a process of analysis and action which they hope will engage everyone in the church. They have proposed that the church maximize and perpetuate the following four social forces: the quest for peace in the world, racial equality, economic justice especially toward the poor, and respect for life from cradle to grave.

What the bishops suggest for everyone in the church is:

(1) that we study their analyses of the major social challenges, which are found in the following pastoral letters: *Brothers and Sisters Together, The Challenge of Peace: God's Promise and Our Response, Catholic Social Teaching and the U.S. Economy;*

(2) that we create forums for dialogue about these and other issues relevant to our communities; and

(3) that we act on the promptings of the Spirit to respond to these problems as best we can with the support of our local Christian communities.

These action and reflection steps are already being taken in many collaborative relationships between laity and religious, as evident in the examples given above. This positive response to the challenge of the bishops makes room for the abandoned and holds promise for the revitalization of religious life and the emergence of the laity as a spiritual force in society.

Effective collaboration between religious and laity provides both a forum for dialogue and a communal base for action on contemporary social problems and the troubles of individuals to which they give rise.

Discussion Questions

1. In your view, which of the criteria for effective lay-religious bonding are most valuable?

2. Would you add any other criteria? How are the criteria you have added similar to those mentioned in this chapter?

3. If you are planning a collaborative venture or evaluating an already-existing one, how well does the venture in question meet the criteria for effective bonding?

4. In which ways could you improve the quality of lay-religious bonding within your collaborative venture?

Footnotes

1. Marie Augusta Neal, S.N.D., "Who They Are and What They Do: Current Forms of Religious Life in the U.S. Church," in RELIGIOUS LIFE IN THE U.S. CHURCH, edited by Robert Daly and others (N.J.: Paulist Press, 1984), pp. 164-165. Neal's "Sisters' Survey" of 1980 shows that 60 percent are ready for work that alleviates the results of poverty; 40 percent for work that eliminates its causes. It also shows that sisters are not satisfied with fulfilling corporate goals within profit-making systems unless the work that they are doing is indeed "the work that Jesus did."

2. Criteria are helpful whenever religious and laity are reflecting about what kind of relationship they want to foster. The term "criteria," as used in this context, refers to the kind of collaborative relationship toward which laity and religious together wish to strive.

3. VATICAN II, THE CHURCH IN THE MODERN WORLD, paragraph #1.

4. "The earliest communities [of Franciscans] had included a large, and even predominant lay element; but laymen disappeared from Franciscan convents very quickly for the same reasons that they had disappeared from communities of earlier religious orders: it was in every way easier to organize and support a religious community if all its members were in holy orders. Besides, the higher aims of preaching, evangelization, and spiritual direction could only be served by the clergy." R. W. Southern, WESTERN SOCIETY AND THE CHURCH IN THE MIDDLE AGES (England: Penguin Books, 1970, pb., 376pp.), p. 351.

5. "The Sisters of St. Joseph... is typical of post-Tridentine congregations which afforded women the opportunity to be religious while taking only simple vows and engaging in active works of the apostolate. As such, it is an early example of its kind, having been established in France in 1651 after communities with similar intentions, such as those begun by Angela Merici, Jane Francis de Chantal and Francis de Sales, Vincent de Paul, and Mary Ward, had been forced to observe the cloister or to employ pious subterfuges—avoiding the title of Sister and replacing perpetual vows with annual promises—in order to retain their freedom of movement." Karen M. Kennelly, C.S.J., "Historical Perspectives on the Experience of Religious Life in the American Church," in RELIGIOUS LIFE IN THE U.S. CHURCH, Robert Daly and others (N.J. Paulist Press, 1984), p. 85.

6. Canon 603: #1. Besides institutes of consecrated life, the Church recognizes the eremitic or anchoritic life by which the Christian faithful devote their life to the praise of God and salvation of the world through a stricter separation from the world, the silence of solitude and assiduous prayer and penance. #2. A hermit is recognized in the law as one dedicated to God in a consecrated life if he or she publicly professes the three evangelical counsels, confirmed by a vow or other sacred bond, in the hands of the diocesan bishop and observes his or her own plan of life under his direction.

Canon 604: #1. Similar to these forms of consecrated life is the order of virgins, who, committed to the holy plan of following Christ more closely, are consecrated to God by the diocesan bishop according to the approved liturgical rite, are betrothed mystically to Christ, the Son of God, and are dedicated to the service of the Church. #2. In order to observe their commitment more faithfully and to perform by mutual support service to the Church which is in harmony with their state these virgins can form themselves into associations.

Canon 605: Approving new forms of consecrated life is reserved to the Apostolic See alone. Diocesan bishops, however, should strive to discern new gifts of consecrated life granted to the Church by the Holy Spirit and they should aid their promoters so that they can express their proposals as well as possible and protect them with suitable statutes, utilizing especially the general norms contained in this section.

7. "This lay spirituality will take its particular character from the circumstances of one's state in life (married and family life, celibacy, widowhood), from one's state of health and from one's professional and social activity." APOSTOLICAM ACUOSITA-TEM, n. 1.

8. Is it not significant that the lay spiritualities which are gaining acceptance among laity are being generated not only by lay people but by clergy and religious as well? Matthew Fox is a Dominican; Henri Nouwen, a priest; Joan Chittester, a Benedictine Sister.

9. "We have seen that for various reasons, both No and Yes are legitimate responses to the question about whether there should be a distinctive spirituality for the laity. A third response would be that we need a lay spirituality for the present time, but that we look forward to the time when this would no longer be necessary. Whatever route is taken, the goal remains clear: to reverence every member of the ecclesial body in his or her unique dignity as a creature of God and to affirm the universal invitation to participate in the fullness of the divine mystery." (p. 207) From Elizabeth A. Dreyer, "A Spirituality for the Laity: Yes or No?", SPIRITUALITY TODAY, Fall 1986, vol. 38, no. 3, pp. 197-208.

10. This author is grateful to Don Kurre of North Platte, NE for his reflections on this topic.

11. For a more developed discussion of laity teaching clergy and religious, see WORK AND FAITH IN SOCIETY: A HANDBOOK FOR DIOCESES AND PARISHES, Maurice L. Monette (Editor), pp. 75-80 (United States Catholic Conference, 1986).

12. This author is grateful to Mary Lou Durall of Silver Spring, MD for her extensive reflections on how religious can better respond to the needs of lay people.

13. The author is grateful to Al and Elise Dirsa of N.H. for their gentle but persuasive reflections.

14. David F. O'Connor, S.T., "Lay Associate Programs: Some Canonical and Practical Considerations," REVIEW FOR RELIGIOUS, March-April, 1985, pp.256-267.

15. Lawrence Cada, S.M. and others, SHAPING THE COMING AGE OF RE-LIGIOUS LIFE (Whitinsville, MA: Affirmation Books, 1979, pb, 196 pp.), p. 47.

16. A useful outline and summary of the social teachings is found in Our Best Kept Secret: THE RICH HERITAGE OF CATHOLIC SOCIAL TEACHING, Michael Schultheis, Edward DeBerri and Peter Henriot, Washington, D.C.: Center of Concern, 1987 (revised, expanded edition), 80 pp.

17. 1971 WORLD SYNOD OF BISHOPS, JUSTICE IN THE WORLD #6.

4

Creating Traditions

Gospel Ventures

History suggests that the vitality of a religious community depends in part on the strategic choice of a concrete project or enterprise which is inspired by the gospel and which responds to the historical needs of the times.[1] The American church has known at least two such gospel ventures: the venture of expanding the Kingdom to newly discovered lands and the venture of building institutions like schools and hospitals for the service of the poor. To some extent these particular ventures are still relevant to historical needs. But, as we saw in earlier chapters, historical needs have shifted in recent times and so has the relevance of former ventures. Some religious communities are discovering new gospel ventures and as a result are being re-vitalized; others are not and some are dying.

Today new gospel ventures are just beginning to surface. People are re-gathering and re-organizing. The formerly strict boundaries of membership in re-vitalized religious institutes are giving way so that other people, lay and clergy, who share an institute's charism and believe in a common gospel venture can organize in response to the new needs of church and society.

Many examples can be found of particular U.S. projects which may in time develop into full-blown gospel ventures for prophetic laity, religious and clergy. Among such projects are the resident community and monastic school at St. Benedict Center in Madison, WI; and social action projects like Peaceworks, Witness for Peace at AVCO, and Catholics Against Nuclear Arms (all mentioned in chapter one). Due to space limitations, I will focus only on four of the many worthy projects which I believe hold promise for lay-religious collaboration: the emerging leadership role of the pastoral administrator, the creation of an American Catholic lay network; the growth of intentional Christian communities; and the evangelization of the unchurched.

The Pastoral Administrator: A New Form of Church Leadership

The Institute for Pastoral Life (IPL) in Kansas City, MO is a response to the contemporary leadership crisis of rural mission dioceses. But, even those of us who work in more resourceful dioceses can identify with the felt need of these rural dioceses.

Predictably, their need will be ours as well. Sooner or later the question will arise: as vocations to male, celibate priesthood continue to decline, how is the church to provide adequate pastoral leadership?

The Institute was created in 1985 precisely in response to the leadership crisis in "home mission dioceses," so-designated by the Chicago-based Catholic Church Extension Society because of an inability to be financially self-supporting and because of a paucity of resources.

The ministerial challenge in these home mission dioceses is to serve a geographically scattered Catholic population with a declining number of priests and few diocesan agencies. IPL's 1984 survey of these dioceses revealed a tremendous variation in the quality and quantity of lay ministry activity and preparation. Respondents generally expressed major dissatisfaction over inadequate training and preparation.

The IPL program is presently in a first phase which consists of training Diocesan Liaison persons who will be responsible for leadership preparation efforts in their own dioceses. So far, 21 Liaisons are participating in a two-year program which focuses on theology of ministry and on leadership training skills. The next phase of the Institute's program is the actual training of lay "Pastoral Administrators" who will be responsible for pastoral leadership in the priestless communities. This training will take place both in Kansas City and in the local dioceses.

There are many reasons why this observer of the scene has chosen IPL as one of the most significant and exciting projects in the U.S. church:

(1) The Institute is squarely facing one of the key issues for the future of the church—leadership. The three bishops who are on the board of IPL and those who have invested personnel in the program perceive that, regardless of their theological positions on ministry, the declining number of priests is compelling them to re-evaluate the processes by which pastoral leaders are chosen and prepared. Supported by the Second Vatican Council's renewed "People of God" ecclesiology, these bishops and the IPL are researching new strategies, within canonical bounds, for providing the local church with quality pastoral leadership. Since this effort is national in scope, no diocese and certainly no home mission diocese need face the leadership crisis alone.

(2) The educational techniques being developed by the Institute will likely be useful for designing the "seminaries" of the future. If the church is to eventually choose leadership from among the faithful who are not necessarily young, celibate, highly educated and male, it will need to create new educational institutions which will rely more heavily on communications technology and educational processes which inte-

grate "home-work" (individual or group study) with "class-work" (study at a central location). If such institutions are to be faithful to Vatican II, they will also need to model the kinds of communication and decision-making processes appropriate to a theology of Baptism which recognizes the calling and giftedness not only of the leaders but of all the faithful as well.

(3) IPL is a strategic, although not a complete response to the present leadership crisis in the U.S. church. Some have critiqued the work of the Institute as failing to deal with the issue of the local Christian community's right to Eucharist. They are right, of course. IPL operates within the present discipline of the church which requires (a) every parish to be under the overall care of a priest-pastor, and (b) every Eucharist to be presided over by an ordained, male, celibate priest. IPL does not question this discipline; it merely works within it. Although the Institute does not deal directly with the right to Eucharist issue, its very existence serves the church by surfacing this crucial issue and by offering a temporary strategy to respond to the church's leadership needs until the time comes when new policies are determined. IPL excites not because it promises to be a permanent institution within the U.S. church, but because it is paving the way for the more responsive institutions of the future.

As the need for pastoral administrators and other new forms of leadership emerges, where and how will these leaders be trained and nurtured? How will ordained clergy be prepared to accept and work with these pastoral administrators? How will parish people be prepared to welcome these lay leaders? Who will attend to these tasks? At this time, the Extension Society, a few bishops, and the Institute have taken the initiative; but as the need grows, who are the prophetic and missionary-spirited people who will respond? This is surely a gospel venture which can inspire lay-religious collaboration in local churches.

The American Catholic Lay Network: A Voice for Laity

The face of a baby does not offer many hints about how the child will look when mature. So it goes for the newly formed American Catholic Lay Network. But already the future looks exciting.

This national lay organization was formed at a convention in Indianapolis in November of 1985. The seventy-plus participants in this "Inter-Regional Planning Meeting" described the major features of their fledgling organization in terms of research, evangelization and networking: (1) Members agreed to research what it means to be lay, American and Catholic. Their spirituality would emerge from the daily experience of family and work. (2) Members would create forums for dialogue between Catholics of all stripes: the driven-away, the emerging, the traditional and the progressives. Such forums would give voice and ownership to the silent laity and empower the creation and spiritual growth of small faith communities. (3) Members would network on four levels: the local (in small communities or in parish-based chapters), the regional, the national and the international. Such networks would facilitate the exchange of information, services, and resources.

In short, the ACLN is, as described in the literature, "an association of people nourished by a lay spirituality, embracing a consistent ethic of life, gathered in small faith communities, and linked by local and national networks."

At present, the organization has a national office in Washington, D.C. and a number of regional groups in cities like Phoenix, South Bend, Washington, D.C., Rochester and St. Louis. Each of these regional groups has organized according to local needs, including faith-sharing, day care, surveying resources for lay formation, seminars on the 1987 Synod on the laity, and forums on justice issues. ACLN also publishes a small-group newsletter called *Gathering*. The bi-monthly paper is sent to all members and is available to unaffiliated subscribers.

The Network is particularly exciting from an educational perspective for several reasons:

(1) ACLN is lay-controlled and oriented to serve particularly lay needs through lay spirituality. Although it is debatable whether a "lay" spirituality should really be all that distinct from one that is clerical or religious, it is historical fact that a paucity of attention has been paid to the lay spiritual experience of family, sexuality, work and civic responsibility. Vatican II preached the holiness of ordinary life. It encouraged laity to assume responsibility for the Christian mission to the world and for the ministry needed to empower that mission within the church. The members of ACLN take the Council seriously and so they also take seriously the evangelizing power of their own experience as laity. Their educational content and approach is lay-centered.

(2) The ACLN provides a home for many Catholics who today feel like spiritual nomads. Spiritual formation, as educators know, is most effective when provided within the context of a community of discourse and service. When such community is absent or weak, spiritual formation is reduced to an intellectual exercise and ignores the human need for modeling, support, challenge and dialogue about personal and social faith concerns. The Network is no mere education program. Its educational context is the small community.

(3) The ACLN is oriented to mission. It is not what Robert Bellah calls a "lifestyle enclave" of like-minded, self-serving individuals. Its culturally-diverse members come from varied positions on the political spectrum with the joint purpose of impacting U.S. society with the faith. Their common study of culture, history and art is directed to action; and their action is directed to the family, to church, and beyond these realms to the social, political and economic. Unlike the goals of too many church education programs, ACLN goals are broader than personal growth, and originate from and are oriented to "doing" and "being" in society.

Pastors and directors of education might encourage the founding of ACLN parish chapters. These chapters could be powerful catalysts for parish adult education and social concern activities. The ACLN admits members of religious institutes on an associate membership basis and sponsors a working committee on lay-religious collaboration. Religious are not being given full membership status at this time so that laity can assume without hesitation the dignity and initiative which has not historically been theirs. But religious are generously funding the organization, encouraging the emergence of the laity, and participating more by "being there" than by leading the way.

The founding and nurture of local chapters of the network is a timely gospel venture in need of lay-religious collaboration.

Intentional Christian Communities

Earthquakes release ancient energies. But they also create homelessness. So it is for many religious and laity who have survived the recent quakes in church and society. They are homeless spirits in a topsy-turvy world looking for a dwelling place where there is a table of food and the good company of friends. Once familiar spiritual havens can no longer contain the life once nurtured within their walls. Well worn spiritual paths have led beyond the familiar and the comfortable. Families are dispersed.

The re-gathering of the church is occuring in some sectors precisely because many no longer feel spiritually at-home. Although most churchgoing Catholics report satisfaction with the spiritual nurture they receive from parish life, many others have left the church entirely or are seeking more than the parish is offering.[2] While the parish serves many as the ordinary structure for the pursuit of holiness, it often fails to serve others who for many reasons are no longer "ordinary" Catholics and who require more extra-ordinary means of holiness. Spiritual homelessness is not an uncommon feeling among such Catholics today whether lay, religious or clergy. Movements like Cursillo, Charismatic Renewal and Marriage Encounter have provided some with a temporary home. Intentional Christian Communities have become home for others, as have other churches. But there are those who still search.

This search for supplementary or even alternative communities of mission and ministry has created bonds of kinship between some of the faithful and the bearers of the "religious community life" tradition which has enriched the life of the church almost since its birth. Age after age, in times of crisis, the church has drawn strength and vigor from new forms of religious community living and their alternative structures for the pursuit of holiness.

The intentional Christian community is surely one of those new forms for the church of today—and members of traditional religious communities are actively promoting it. What are these intentional Christian communities and how do they constitute a gospel venture for lay-religious collaboration?

Since 1968, I have been actively involved with intentional Christian communities in four different cities. In each case, 50 to 200 other people like myself have gathered for purposes like the following: to pray and worship each Sunday with a community small enough for mutual sharing of faith experience; to make sense of daily living in the light of the gospel; to care for each other; and to discern and act upon the needs of people around us. The community has been our "church." It has given us what we could not find in our local parishes.

A more formal description of the intentional Christian community is given to us in what is perhaps the best reference on such communities in the U.S., *Dangerous Memories: House Churches and Our American Story:*

> An intentional Christian community is a relatively small group of persons committed to ongoing conversation and shared action along four distinguishable but interrelated dimensions:

—They are consistently committed to a high degree of mutuality in the relationships among them.
—They pursue an informed critical awareness of and an active engagement within the cultural, political and economic megasystems of their society.
—They cultivate and sustain a network of lively connections with other persons, communities and movements of similar purpose.
—They attend faithfully to the Christian character of their community's life.[3]

Such communities have arisen on every continent during the last thirty years. In the U.S. they are found in almost every metropolitan area.

There are several characteristics which intentional Christian communities and religious institutes hold in common:

1. Both are alternatives. ICC's provide an alternative to the parish for a few people who are serious about pursuing their Christian faith. Religious institutes are an alternative Christian lifestyle.

2. Both stand within the prophetic tradition. In relation to church, ICC's are a new way of being church. They explore forms of leadership, structures of decision-making, liturgical practices, and educational models that are not currently used in the regular parishes. In relation to society, ICC's are especially attentive to social issues and to the needs of the abandoned. As we have seen in chapter two, religious institutes also represent strategic responses to special needs in the church and society.

3. Both ICC's and religious institutes are devoted to the church and tradition. If ICC's and religious institutes do not conform to present church practices, they act, not out of rebelliousness, but out of loyalty to authorities and faithfulness to the tradition.

In my experience, ICC's are models of collaboration between laity and religious. In most cases, both participate equally as members, sharing responsibility for the direction and maintenance of the community. Religious contribute by providing presiders for liturgy, pastoral advice, and counsel; and by linking the community with ecclesial tradition, structures and resources. The very participation of religious sometimes lends needed legitimation and credibility to the community. Collaboration between religious institutes and ICC's, however, is at its best when the status of religious within the wider church is used not as a license to dominate or monopolize the community's life and mission, but as a link with the prophetic tradition of which both are heirs.

If Christians continue to search for more intense ways of growing in faith, it is not unlikely that the intentional Christian community will become a more widespread phenomenon. It may eventually be adopted as an official pastoral strategy, as the basic Christian community has in countries like Brazil. In any case, the ICC is one of many possible strategies for the re-gathering and re-evangelization of the U.S. church. If more widely adopted, the ICC strategy will require a new corps of men and women who will provide training for lay pastoral leaders and ordained clergy.

Evangelization of the Unchurched

It was not so long ago that words like mission and missionary referred mainly to the work of priests and religious institutes in foreign lands. They invoked images of poor people in under-developed countries being catechized by foreign missionaries. But now such words are being used in reference to the work needed in the U.S. itself, in ordinary parishes, even in suburbia.

A new type of missionary work is needed: the pre-evangelization (or preliminary evangelization) of the unchurched. It is estimated that there are in the U.S. over 80 million unchurched. These include both the not-yet Christian and the no-longer Christian, that is, those who

have not believed in Christ and those no longer practicing. A "missionary situation" is developing here as it has in Europe. Significant groups
of people are standing outside the church. Their situation is calling for
persons who can systematically pass across the boundaries of the Christian community and announce Christ again to those far from him, with
new methods and in a new language. At a time when foreign missions
are coming to an end, home missions are starting up. This new "mission" calls for a new kind of "missionary." In the words of a respected
futurologist,

> It can be said without exaggeration that the "Christian West"
> has become the most difficult mission area. Evangelization of
> persons alienated from the church cannot be expected of
> priests, who are already too few. They can at most be anim-
> ators, encouraging and prompting the laity. What once applied
> to all disciples of Christ ought again to become self-evident:
> every Christian a "missionary."[4]

This gospel venture requires a new corps of "missionaries" who can
draw appropriate lessons from the traditional missionary ventures of the
religious institutes and move beyond. The challenge is to recognize and
appreciate the human values of the unchurched; make contact with
them on the common ground of humanity; detect and interpret their
longings for fulfillment and answer them with Christian hope.

A Word About Limits

Given their historical situation, it is easier for many religious institutes to develop an impressive mission statement than to make strategic
choices about gospel ventures. A provincial council of sisters once told
me how proud they were of the mission statement they had written. In
the same breath they revealed that the average age of the sisters was 68
and that they had not had a novice in 12 years. A council member in her
forties said that the sisters referred to her as one of the young ones.
Mission statements can be ideal but unrealistic.

"Spiritual grandparenting" is the metaphor I used for the task of these sisters as a province. They took consolation in that image. Why not? Consider the task. Grandparents have done their work as parents: they have raised their immigrant-church children, nurturing them through the Second Vatican Council, standing by during the crisis of spiritual adolescence, so that now they can be comforted that many of these children have developed a self-identity of being called and gifted. Of course, the work of a parent is never done. Generativity is also the task of grandparents. Now they need to coach from afar as their children nurture the next generation. Their wisdom is useful and welcomed by some. Their shoulders are needed for the inevitable tears. Their faith and hope witness to the worthwhileness of being and caring for church.

It is unrealistic to expect a grandparent to raise yet another generation. Some grandparent religious institutes still insist on trying. But even if the mission is clear the resources are meager. Unrealistic self-images inevitably lead to disappointment.

Some lay people get the definite impression that certain bonding efforts of religious are like the clutching of a drowning man. They want no part in such a relationship because it will only bring them down. They are right, aren't they? Painfully right perhaps, especially if the institute is frantically grasping for recruits or attempting to liven-up a dwindling community with the presence of outsiders.

Surely there is a special grace for grandparents. Perhaps it is the grace to both embrace one's limits and live in anticipation and thanksgiving for the birth of new life. When such grace is operative, bonding relationships are not clutching, but freeing. Laity sense that they are being given both room to grow and access to traditional wisdom.

Granted that there are limits to the contribution of aging religious communities, there also exists a vitality to be maximized across religious communities through the networking of younger men and women religious who can be, along with other faithful, a creative force in the recreating of the church. This vitality, as well as the vitality of the laity, also needs the loving nurture of our religious grandparents.

Teamwork and Sabbath

This book has been written for Christians who see that the church in our time is being re-invented and are concerned about the shape of the church to come. It has focused on the new spirit of friendship that is oc-curing between laity and members of religious institutes. It has attemp-ted to name the new dimensions of that relationship (Chapter I), to situ-ate it within a history of Christian ideals (Chapter II), to offer criteria for evaluating and planning collaborative projects (Chapter III), and finally to highlight a few of the most exciting contemporary Gospel ven-tures.

The re-invention of the church in response to the signs of the times is occuring all over the world and, if an eminent church futurologist is right, will probably continue for the next twenty years.[5] We who care about the future of the church can each in our own way shape the church of the next millennium. But all of this talk about shaping, rein-venting, planning and collaborating is babble (and Babel) if taken out of the context of God's initiative.

In the midst of social and ecclesial earthquakes, rest is as necessary as rebuilding. Perhaps more so, because the busybody who never stops too easily misinterprets the blueprints and hence loses perspective on the task. Without perspective, the rebuilding may well be in vain. With-out rest, the inevitable frustrations become unbearable.

If the new spirit of friendship between laity and religious is marked by mutuality and teamwork, so is our relationship with the God who is rebuilding the church. For God's initiative is at the very root of the crisis of our times. Is it not our belief that God is calling us to rebuild? That God's Spirit erupted into Vatican II? That God brought the work of the immigrant American church into fruition? If so, our relationship to God is one of teamwork, and teamwork means coordinating efforts. Coordinating efforts is impossible without prayer time.

The builders of the church to come are a Sabbath people, highly skilled in resting, playing and talking with God about the day's work. Out of Sabbath comes grace-filled work, new and energizing perspectives on the task, and greater resolve to respond to the greater needs. The re-invention of the church is not a tedious, frustrating, and solitary task, but an exciting venture which all the baptized share with a God of grace and surprise.

Discussion Questions

1. In what "gospel venture(s)" has your lay group and/or religious community historically been involved?

2. How responsive is your group's gospel venture to the needs of today's most abandoned?

3. What new gospel ventures give you hope for the future of prophetic community life?

4. What, in your view, are the most favorable conditions for the emergence of new styles of lay-religious bonding? What kinds of Christian community life do you predict will emerge in the next twenty years?

Footnotes

1. "Religious communities which have a significant positive impact on the church and the world and which have committed membership are characterized by a dynamic integration of a gospel venture, of the appropriate modes of organizing, and of the persons

who are members of the community." Lawrence Cada, S.M. and others, SHAPING THE COMING AGE OF RELIGIOUS LIFE (Whitinsville, MA: Affirmation Books, 1979, pb, 196pp.), p. 95.

2. For data on the state of the parish, see the NOTRE DAME STUDY OF CATH-OLIC PARISH LIFE. Reports are published bimonthly. Inquiries by telephone: (219) 239-7212 or 239-5510.

3. DANGEROUS MEMORIES: HOUSE CHURCHES AND OUR AMERICAN STORY, Bernard J. Lee and Michael A. Cowan, Kansas City: Sheed & Ward, 1986, pp. 91-92.

4. Walbert Bühlmann THE CHURCH OF THE FUTURE: A MODEL FOR THE YEAR 2001. Maryknoll, N.Y.: Orbis Books, 1986, p. 11.

5. Bühlmann, p. 115.

Home delivery
from
Sheed & Ward

Here's your opportunity to have bestsellers delivered right to you. Our free catalog is filled with the newest titles on spirituality, church in the modern world, women in religion, ministry, small group resources, adult education/scripture, medical ethics videos and Sheed & Ward classics.

Please send me a free Sheed & Ward catalog for home delivery.

NAME _____

ADDRESS _____

CITY _____ STATE/ZIP _____

If you have friends who would like to order books at home, we'll send them a catalog to —

NAME _____

ADDRESS _____

CITY _____ STATE/ZIP _____

NAME _____

ADDRESS _____

CITY _____ STATE/ZIP _____